You Can

Have It All,

Just Not at the

Same Damn Time

PORTFOLIO
PENGUIN

You Can Have It All, Just Not at the Same Damn Time

ROMI NEUSTADT

Portfolio / Penguin
An imprint of Penguin Random House LLC
penguinrandomhouse.com

Most Portfolio books are available at a discount when purchased in quantity for
sales promotions or corporate use. Special editions, which include personalized
covers, excerpts, and corporate imprints, can be created when purchased in
large quantities. For more information, please call (212) 572-2232 or
e-mail specialmarkets@penguinrandomhouse.com. Your local
bookstore can also assist with discounted bulk purchases using the Penguin
Random House corporate Business-to-Business program. For assistance in
locating a participating retailer, e-mail B2B@penguinrandomhouse.com.

Library of Congress Cataloging-in-Publication Data
Names: Neustadt, Romi, author.
Title: You can have it all, just not at the same damn time / Romi Neustadt.
Description: [New York] : Portfolio / Penguin, [2020] |
Includes bibliographical references. |
Identifiers: LCCN 2019034472 (print) | LCCN 2019034473 (ebook) |
ISBN 9780593085950 (hardcover) | ISBN 9780593085967 (ebook)
Subjects: LCSH: Women—Life skills guides. | Self-actualization
(Psychology) | Success—Psychological aspects. | Work-life balance. |
Quality of life. | Work and family.
Classification: LCC HQ1221 .N48 2020 (print) | LCC HQ1221 (ebook) |
DDC 305.4—dc23
LC record available at https://lccn.loc.gov/2019034472
LC ebook record available at https://lccn.loc.gov/2019034473

Paperback ISBN: 9780593853948

Book design by Amanda Dewey

147141878

For every woman with big dreams who wants to live a fulfilled,
authentic life without feeling stressed, exhausted, inadequate,
or batshit crazy. This is my love letter to you.

And for the woman I'm raising. Bebe,
may you always stay true to who you are
and go after what's important to you.
And always lead with love.

Contents

Introduction

We women are suffering from a dangerous and somewhat debilitating condition called unrealistic expectations. We contract it from each other, our critics, our cultural history, the voices in our heads, and Instagram. We walk around with this idea of who we're supposed to be, how much we're supposed to accomplish, and how we're supposed to look while we're doing it. Raise kind, smart, well-adjusted kids who make us proud and contribute to society. Build a career that's lucrative and fulfilling and meaningful. Nurture a vibrant and supportive romantic partnership. Maintain flourishing friendships and be a joiner, a doer, and an influencer in our community. Maintain a clean, clutter-free, and inviting home and a healthy weight. And keep up with the ever-growing list of required personal hygiene practices.

We're helping to spread this epidemic by all of us walking around trying to act like everything's OK. We're skillfully juggling all our balls in the air, messy buns perched on our heads in quiet defiance to the laws of scalp oil. It's only when we let our guards down that we admit how we really feel.

It's in our Facebook comments of "Yasssss!" and "Amen!" we add to the post that talks about how we're barely holding our shit together. It's in the weary glances we give one another as we load our groceries into our trunks, while simultaneously trying to keep our kids from killing each other and accomplish something on a work call. It's in the mass ugly cry that ensues when we get together for a glass of wine, and the conversation turns to how we're really feeling.

We're stressed out. We feel like failures. We're not doing the things we really want to do. And we're tired. Really fucking tired.

We're trying to **Have It All**, but we're going about it all wrong. I know this idea has been brutally beat up and called a myth. I almost believed it too. Years ago, when I was in my thirties, I was watching *The Oprah Winfrey Show*, and my idol Oprah said that it was impossible for women to Have It All. The conversation was about long-term relationships, children, and career. I can't remember who the woman was that she was talking to or the exact words she used, but Oprah argued that it's impossible to flourish in all three areas, and she credited her ability to do what she'd done because she didn't have kids. That really stuck with me, haunted me even. And I remember thinking at the time, "That can't be true. There's got to be a way to have it all." I love Oprah, but I had to prove her wrong because I refused to accept that my dreams weren't possible.

Turns out, my dream life was possible, and I've worked really hard to figure out how to make it happen. Throughout the last ten years of juggling a marriage, raising two kids, being a helpful daughter to an aging mom, building an eight-figure business, being a somewhat active member of the communities I care about, and keeping myself healthy and able to fit into my jeans, I've acquired and created the tools to Have It All without going batshit crazy. And I'm excited to share them with you in this book.

I've figured out why this concept has gotten such a bad rap. People have been confusing **Having It All** with **Doing It All**. You or I most certainly cannot Do It All. We can't be all things to all people, live a life of Shoulds, have a never-ending to-do list, accomplish what we actually want to during our precious time on Earth, and not be stressed out of our minds, exhausted, or worse. It's not possible.

It is possible, however, to have all the things that are really important to us. How do I know? Because I've done it, and I've made it my mission to help other women do it too.

I've been privileged to spend the last decade working with women of all different backgrounds, ages, shapes, professional pedigrees, and confidence levels. We were all brought together in a common goal of building businesses of our own through a direct sales company that's grown to be the number one skincare brand in North America. Because of my desire to change my life, my tenacity, my love for helping others grow, and a considerable amount of luck, I became a mentor and a coach to tens of thousands of women on our team. And when I wrote a book entitled *Get Over Your Damn Self* about how to build a business like mine, I got to meet thousands more.

From stay-at-home moms to working out-of-home moms, from badass corporate chicks to small business owners, from new college grads to retired empty nesters, from elementary school teachers to physicians, I've had the unique opportunity to learn about women's dreams for their lives and their frustration over not realizing them. They've shared their short-term goals and long-term big, hairy, audacious ones and all the reasons why they can't reach them. And I've had a front-row seat to many who've overcome all the reasons why they should fail and instead triumphed, often far beyond what they ever thought was possible. For years people have told me some variation of the following: "I don't know how you do what you do.... You're superhuman.... I could never do what you do." These expressions of resigned defeat have fueled my other relentless pursuit—to help others design the lives they really want too.

I'm obsessed with the following questions:

> Why do some women become the people they were designed to be and create the lives they really want to live, and others don't?

> Why is it so hard for all of us—yes, me included—to do the things we *really* want to do, become the people we *really* want to be?

> Why do some of us make big strides, experience breakthroughs and success, but then stop in our evolution or even slide backward?

I've been able to leave two careers that were no longer serving me (law and PR). I found my professional calling, built a wildly successful business, and became a bestselling, award-winning author. I'm one half of a sixteen-year marriage that's still going strong and raising two spectacular kids (actually, they're raising me). I've conquered body issues and self-doubt and family drama and illness to become the healthiest I've ever been—both physically and emotionally. I live a life that I really love *nearly* every single day (I mean, c'mon, some days just make you want to pull your hair out no matter how much you've got your shit together).

But what my life has evolved into is not the result of super-powers or figuring out how to survive on less sleep (just the opposite, in fact). It's not because things are easier for me, or I've somehow insulated myself from all the things that plague *other* women. Like you, as I grew up, my life got cluttered with Shoulds, never-ending internal and external chatter, and endless to-do lists. The more successful I became, the more the Shoulds and chatter multiplied, and the longer my to-do lists became. It was effing up my quest to keep reaching my goals, while still being a fulfilled, happy, and peaceful human in the process. I had to figure out how to get the most out of my precious time on Earth and how to do the things I wanted to do in all parts of my life.

That's what this book is all about. That and, more important for you, how you can learn from my experiences and road-weathered wisdom and take the tools I've collected and created and apply them to your life.

You won't be able to Have It All overnight; I sure as hell didn't. And let me be crystal clear—your All may look very different from mine and very different from the woman next to you in yoga, ahead of you in line at the grocery store, and in the office next to yours at work. As you get to know me, you might think, "Good lord, I sure don't want to live her life." Good for you! I want you to figure out what you really want for *your* life, what makes *you* happy, fulfilled, and at peace.

I readily admit that I don't have all the answers. Confession: I haven't yet mastered all the strategies, tools, mindset tweaks, and habits I talk about in the pages ahead. I still work on all of it every single day because—like you—I'm a work in progress. It reminds me of a fabulous meme I saw on Instagram: "Just because I give you advice, it doesn't mean I know more than you. It just means I've done more stupid shit." But I really believe that if you come on this journey with me—if you go *All In*—you're going to come out on the other side with a new way of looking at your life and what you want and how to go get it.

I'm asking you to dig deep, be brutally honest with yourself, and invest the time to do the exercises. If you do, by the end of this book, you will be able to zone in on what really matters to you, so you can ditch everything that isn't serving your dreams. You'll recognize and embrace your worth, which will dictate where you spend your time. You'll create habits that will protect your time and energy. You'll show up as the real you in all parts of your life. You'll learn to push aside the fears that keep you from being who you were designed to be. And you'll have a lot more grace with yourself, because you deserve that just as much as you deserve to Have It All.

This book is for every woman who has dreams and unlimited potential and wants to live a fulfilled, authentic life. So, basically, all of us. We just need a little help figuring out what to do and what not to do. That's why I'm here, Sister.

Here's to you and me exploring the lessons I've learned that changed and continues to change my life. They can change yours too.

Let's go!

XO,

Romi

You Can

Have It All,

Just Not at the

Same Damn Time

One

FOCUS, BABY, FOCUS

*My mind is like someone emptied the kitchen
junk drawer onto a trampoline.*

—Most women and a very clever Instagram meme

⌐

There's a woman, let's call her Jane, who wakes up in the morning and races out of bed to get dressed and put on her makeup—a difficult task with too-tired eyes from too little sleep—to get a head start on the daily morning dance of kid chaos. She gulps coffee and scans email and feeds the dogs and herds her kids and herself out into the day.

She tries to slay her job so she'll get that promotion, while her mind darts from what she's going to cook for dinner, to how to fit in a workout before picking up one kid from practice and the other from tutoring, to the latest snarky text from her friend, to how she's going to get out of the baby shower she doesn't want to go to and the committee she doesn't want to sit on, to what she'll possibly have left over for her husband tonight. Oh, and how many emails she thinks she can get to after dinner.

Then, late at night, after everyone has gone to bed and taken their relentless requests of her with them, she becomes one with the couch, a big bag of popcorn, and the remote. The rhythmic chewing and clicking for the perfect mind-numbing Netflix choice aren't quite enough to keep her from feeling the feelings.

She can't believe that another week, month, year has whizzed by, and she still hasn't gotten to her really big goals, like writing that novel and daily meditation and losing twenty pounds so she can fit into the clothes she keeps in the "One Day" section of her closet. Hell, she can't even get to her little goals of organizing her closet and getting quarterly bikini waxes, which everyone knows are not nearly enough.

She's exhausted, overwhelmed, and afraid someone or everyone is going to figure out she's winging it all the time. She's so tired of pretending she's got it all under control. And her biggest fear is that another week, month, year is going to whizz by and on the couch she'll sit, lamenting that she doesn't know where all the time is going and that she's not becoming who she was meant to be, not living the life she really wants to live.

I bet you can empathize with Jane. You might even be Jane. Let's be real: at some point, we're all Jane.

We're living reactive lives, which means that all the things coming at us every single day get our attention before the stuff we actually planned to do. And the stuff we planned to do keeps getting pushed to the bottom of the to-do list, sometimes hanging out there so long that we forget why we really wanted to do it in the first place. Or, even worse, we've convinced ourselves that it was a stupid idea or beyond our abilities.

There's so much coming at us at any given moment, so many tabs open on our laptops and in our brains. Is it any wonder we

don't know what to do for the next five minutes, let alone the next
five months? Or five years?

You've likely heard this gem: "Where your attention goes your
energy flows." It's the God's honest truth. How many times have
you set aside something that's important to you to answer a phone
call or a text, field a request for help from a co-worker or one of
your kids, dropped everything for an all-company email or school
newsletter? And then you try to get back to what you wanted to
be doing in the first place, but you've lost your flow, your mojo,
your willpower—whatever you had, it's gone—and you say your
favorite version of "Screw it, I'll do it tomorrow." And just like
that, your day of best intentions has turned into a day you'll settle
for. Instead of moving your life forward, you'll cross off a bunch
of things on your to-do list that aren't really that impactful. But
damn, it does feel good to accomplish *something*.

How does it happen? It's because our **Focus** is misplaced.
Where we Focus our time, energy, thoughts, and actions defines
our life and who we are. Whatever we Focus on is what gets bigger. Whether it's a dream, a goal, a feeling, or a zit. What we think
about all day is what we manifest. So we have to make sure that
we're Focusing on the right stuff.

If our Focus is on the gazillion bits from the kitchen junk
drawer, we're not really Focusing at all. We're reacting to life,
instead of living it. But when we Focus on what's really important
to us and ignore the rest, we live intentional, successful, and fulfilled lives.

I learned about the power of Focus when I was building my
direct sales business. On paper, I shouldn't have been successful
because one could argue I had too much on my plate. I had a busy
PR consultancy. Nate was three, Bebe was six months old, and I

was helping John with his medical practice (he's a naturopathic doctor). My mom was growing older and facing more and more health challenges. I was trying to be active in the community, and I was trying to lose baby weight (which, it turns out, was a two-year project for me). We were shouldering financial burdens; despite a two-professional household, we weren't able to save for retirement or college funds, and we sure didn't have much of an emergency cushion in case the shit hit the fan. And we didn't have time freedom because we were both tied to the fee-for-service model and the billable hour—if we didn't work, we didn't get paid.

In spite of my very full plate, John and I agreed that I simply couldn't say no to a chance to grow my own turn-key business with an established, well-respected brand. So I jumped in.

I soon figured out that what might seem like a ridiculous amount for any one human to take on was actually doable, *if* I got very picky about where I spent my time and practiced grace with myself. I got laser-like focused on the most important things to me and why they were so important: our kids, who deserved a present, loving mom; building my new business, which would set me and John free; and staying healthy so I could do what I really wanted to do and enjoy the journey. I didn't do volunteer work, I wasn't the classroom mom, I declined to renew my gig as the preschool Hebrew school teacher. I didn't have a lot of non-biz-related social time. I didn't watch TV or read *People* magazine (because I quickly learned I could get income-producing work done on the toilet). I chose sleep over sex most of the time (it's OK, I've since made it up to him and myself, thank you very much). I was focused and intentional and proactive with my time.

I understood that there were only so many hours in the day, that I had only so much energy and bandwidth that I had to Focus on what was going to get me where I wanted to be—as a mom, as an entrepreneur, as a healthy human. I had blinders on, and it worked.

In six months, I stepped away from my award-winning PR career. In a little over a year, I became one of the most successful people in the company I work with, and in less than two and a half years, our life dramatically changed. John was able to leave clinical practice, become more of a hands-on dad, and put all his professional efforts into his dietary supplement start-up. We were able to move from Montana to our dream location of San Diego, with both of us working on our fast-growing businesses from home around our fast-growing kids. We could afford housecleaning and an incredible nanny whenever we needed her and date nights and blow outs (well, I got the blow outs). This all happened because I learned how to Focus.

ABF: ALWAYS BE FOCUSING

So I had it all figured out, right? The rest of my life was destined to be nirvana, with ease and efficiency and bluebirds landing on my shoulders as I whistled my way through continuing to build an empire, raise two uber-dynamic kids (empirically speaking, of course), and be a beacon of physical health and spiritual fulfillment and a loving wife who routinely throws her hubs a bone.

Not.

See, here's the thing: the more successful we become, the more responsibilities we shoulder and the bigger our dreams get, the more our minds turn into kitchen junk drawers on trampolines. The more we become overwhelmed by the unrelenting onslaught of things that we think we need to do, goals we need to set, people we need to touch, and places we need to be. The more we forget to do the very things, practice the very habits and disciplines that brought us success in the first place. We forget to Focus.

As my success grew exponentially, so did my stress. Not enough time to do the things that really moved the needle on my business. Not enough time and energy for my most important people—John and the kids. Not enough time and energy on myself, in order to stay healthy in my body, mind, and spirit. Not enough time and energy on other projects that were gnawing on my soul to give birth to. And not enough time and energy spent enjoying the life I had worked so hard to create.

Then one day I heard Tony Robbins say something that hit me so hard. One of those moments of great epiphany that, if I were a cartoon character, I would've been struck by a bolt of lightning and come to with an enormous smile, frizzed-out electrocuted hair, and an index finger pointing straight to the sky. Tony said:

> *"If you're stressed in your business,*
> *you're a business operator,*
> *not a business owner."*

It was what Oprah would call an *Aha Moment* (see, I told you I love Oprah). I was approaching my business not as a CEO should, but as an employee reporting to a job. I wasn't being strategic and meticulous about where I spent my time.

But I didn't stop there. I took it one step further than Tony. I came to terms with the fact that I not only wasn't owning my business, I wasn't owning my life. And that's why I started my business in the first place! I decided right then and there to figure out how I was going to take control of this monster I had created.

I had to make a decision, the same decision I'm asking you to make, no matter where you're at in your personal or professional life:

Do I want to be a hot mess who's stressed out, unfulfilled, unable to find the joy in my journey, and unable to slow down the speed of my precious time on Earth?

Or do I want to be a badass and balanced ladyboss and love my life?

I started reading and listening to everything I thought would help. I started having unfiltered and uninterrupted conversations with John. And it led me to a few discoveries. First, I realized I needed to devote a significant amount of time and effort to figure out where to spend my energy. But this wouldn't be about time management. It would be about finding the soul of my life. I needed to start caring only about the things that deeply mattered to me. I needed to say "fuck it" to everything that wasn't truly important and put my time and energy into the things that truly were. I was Focusing on all the wrong stuff: trying to be everything to everyone, trying to please everyone, and trying to live up to what others expected of me (or what I thought they expected of me). Not to mention allowing myself to get derailed by other people's issues and drama. It was time for me to Focus again on what mattered.

But what really mattered to me? I had become reactive, so busy getting shizz done that I had lost touch with what was driving me. What was it that I wanted to work toward?

Since these are the questions that the women I work with have a hard time answering, I'm guessing you do too. But don't worry, I'm going to help you find your answers. And I'm going to help you stop living like the ball in a pinball machine.

"You need to Focus!" isn't new to you. You've seen it a gazillion times on an inspirational poster or in a how-to article. You get its importance, but you haven't had the tools. Focus isn't a mere declaration. It's a daily practice that each of us must master, and it involves an array of new behaviors and beliefs—confronting the unhelpful and unhealthy thoughts, fears, and habits—and cultivating discipline. It also requires that you be bold and brave and selfish enough to declare—to quote the Spice Girls—what you want, what you really, really want.

So let's help you figure that out.

Two

LIVE BY YOUR ONE WORD

We either live with intention or exist by default.

—Kristin Armstrong, three-time
Olympic gold medalist

⌐

About seven years ago, I was living my very full, #blessed, and successful life, and I was so #grateful. But, to review, I was an exhausted hot mess. I knew I had to change where I was focusing my time, but I didn't know how. It's one thing to declare you're going to Focus on what really matters to you. It's a whole other thing to *know* what really matters to you. And this tired, weary working mama who was trying to grow a biz, nurture a family, and make a difference didn't know what I really wanted anymore.

I figured it out when I ran away from home.

About seven years ago, I went to John and said, "I need a selfish long weekend away from you, the kids, the team, my mom, everything." And off to Las Vegas I went, because I knew I needed to lock myself into a very lovely suite and figure out how I was going to do this. How I was going to take control over my life and get to the next level of authentic, purpose-filled living. With less bitchiness, exhaustion, and stressed out–ness.

Now, let me stop right here and be perfectly clear: I'm not suggesting you run away from home. And I fully appreciate that many of you reading this can't grab a flight to Vegas and put yourself up at the Four Seasons. You're thrilled if you get the bathroom to yourself for forty-five minutes without someone banging on the door. But stick with me, because I want to share with you the strategy and methodology that I came up with that helped not only me but also the thousands of others I've coached, no Vegas suite required.

If you learn anything from my experience, it should be this undeniable truth: if we can be more intentional with our most precious resources of time, energy, emotions, and mindset, which will reduce our feelings of stress and being overwhelmed, we can be more productive and more fulfilled humans. We'll feel more confident and empowered to live our truth. We'll lead with love instead of fear. Imagine what that will do, not only for our lives but for the lives of everyone we love, serve, work and play with, and parent. And trust me, if you can master this stuff before you really hit the big time, all the better.

THE POWER OF ONE WORD

So back to that long weekend in December, to the suite at the Four Seasons. In the stillness, cozied up in a fluffy robe and surrounded by the tools for my transformation—my laptop, a new notebook with some kind of inspirational cover, and a let's-get-to-work-on-you messy bun, I stumbled upon the concept of the *One Word*. This was a few years before the Word of the Year movement was so in vogue. Before there were those cute little washer bracelets that were on the *Today* show. I had never heard of this concept before, but it really resonated with me. So I started figuring out the One Word that would encapsulate the coming year for me. It would be my guidepost for the whole year—personally, professionally, emotionally, spiritually... all the -allys. This would be so much more powerful than New Year's resolutions, which usually end up as a neglected list of failures and disappointments by mid-February. It's not just me who fails at resolutions; studies have shown that as few as 8 percent are actually kept.

The word I settled on in solitude in that Vegas suite was *Balance*. As long as I can remember, I've been what is commonly referred to as type A. I do. I accomplish. I produce. I set goals, and I hit 'em. Get the A. Get into a good college and graduate with the top honors in my department. Get into a top ten law school and nab a sought-after lawyer gig. Switch careers and move up the ladder and win awards for my work. You get the point.

And I'm the type of type A who is very competitive—not with others, mind you, but with myself, relentlessly so. Constantly pushing myself to go beyond where I've been before. To quote Lady Gaga, I was born this way. And it was certainly nurtured and exacerbated by a mother with unrelenting perfectionist tendencies and a mild case of OCD. I grew up going from one goal to the next, a never-ending series of sprints to the summit, followed by short-yet-destructive crashes until I could muster the energy and focus to accomplish the next thing.

It was this way that I approached being an entrepreneur. Sales is a very seductive drug for type As like me. Goals that reset every month. Always something more to accomplish. A hierarchy to ascend. Recognition for a job well done. And, like pretty much every entrepreneurial venture, there's always more work to do, people to help, business to build.

Don't get me wrong: I'm in part very grateful for my type A, obsessive way with which I built my business. I'll never know whether I would've experienced the fast success I did had I done it differently. But more than four years into my business, I decided to devote 2013 to finally learning how to live in Balance.

What did that mean to me? To not live in an endless series of all-consuming sprints, but to find joy every day among the to-dos and goals and chaos and have the kind of life I really wanted. As I told my team and my blog readers then, "Because if I don't, all this money and all this freedom are going to be wasted."

Whether you're reading this toward the end of the year, in January, or in any month in between, figure out what your One Word is. It encapsulates your intention; what you want to work on, experience, accomplish, give, and receive. It's your guidepost, your personal mantra for the rest of this year and/or the upcoming one.

And it's not what you think it *should* be. Your One Word must speak to your heart, your soul. Only you can determine what it is, because only you know what you truly want.

My One Word Is . . .

....

What it means to me:

....

....

....

Your One Word should become so much a part of you and your being over the next twelve months that you could tattoo it on your wrist. Now, I'm not saying you should, but that's how ever-present it should be. Or get yourself one of those cute washer bracelets. (No, I do not profit whatsoever from the sale of those bracelets, but they sure are cool. And I've filed them under my ever-growing list of "Why didn't I think of that?")

BUT IT TAKES MORE THAN DECLARING ONE WORD

I knew that just declaring my One Word wasn't going to be the magic elixir to get more out of life without becoming more of a basket case. More Googling, reading, and quiet time for thinking led me to a process that I took myself through that long weekend in December, a process that I've taken my team and readers of my blog through every January since. And now it's your turn.

Once we figure out our One Word, we have to establish our *Priorities* that serve it, which will influence where we put our time, effort, and attention. Now, if you've picked up this book and are trying to figure out how to get more out of life, you're likely an overachiever. We overachievers may think we're supposed to have a laundry list of Priorities, but we're not. The point is to

Focus on, as the definition of priority dictates, that which is more important than anything else. Our Priorities are our values, lifestyle, principles, and beliefs that are so important to us right now that not serving them is nonnegotiable. And because they're the most important things to us right now, we must declare them in the present tense.

After establishing our Priorities, we get to set our *Goals*— both short- and long-term—that serve our Priorities. It's important to understand how Goals are different. While our Priorities are what's most important and meaningful in our lives today, our Goals are things that haven't yet been realized, but we're committed to making them happen.

For example, let's say that you're not super thrilled with the apartment you're renting because of inadequate space or loud neighbors, and you really want to buy a house. One of your Priorities might be "I live in a home I love." A Goal to serve that Priority might be to save a certain amount of money every month this year to amass the down payment you'll need to buy your own house. Another Goal to serve that Priority could be to make double batches every time you cook to fill your freezer with food you can bring for lunch instead of getting takeout. Or maybe one of your Priorities is "I love the work I do and who I get to do it with," but you're not finding that in your current job. So a Goal to serve that Priority would be to go on one networking lunch a week to explore other opportunities. Or, like so many of the women I work with who want to become their own bosses, to work their side hustle every day to grow it into an exit ramp.

Here's what's so important about this relationship. If our Goals don't support our Priorities, we feel off, scattered, stressed, and unfulfilled. Sound familiar? That happens because we're not living our truth. So I'm asking you to invest the time to really soul search your Priorities and then align your Goals with them.

Just as I curb my inner overachiever to keep the number of Priorities manageable, each year I set an absolute maximum of five Goals per Priority, and I encourage you to do the same. Unless you've found that elusive pill that gives you more than twenty-four hours in a day and no need for sleep.

So let's go back to my very first year of this experiment to illustrate how this whole process works. Remember, my One Word was Balance.

My Priorities in service of Balance were:

· I make healthy decisions.

· I am building a fast-growing business without working more hours.

· I am engaged and present in the lives of my husband and kids.

These are the three things that were most important to me back then, and I took a leap of faith that if I lived my life every day with these as the Focus, I would get much closer to living in the Balance I so desperately craved. The Goals that served my Priority of making healthy decisions were:

· Exercise five times a week, doing a variety of workouts to make it fun and avoid injuries.

· Keep washed and cut up fruits and vegetables on hand every week to grab for snacks and to add to meals.

· Go to bed at 10:00 p.m. during the week to get more sleep.

· Do something fun every week.

Goals that served my business-building Priority included:

· Devote six hours a week to mentoring the hardest-working team members with the most promising growth potential.
· Create a more collaborative team leadership that empowers and showcases my most successful team members.

Goals that served my Priority of being engaged and present for my most important peeps included:

· Commit to one-on-one alone time (twenty to sixty minutes) with each child every week.
· Commit to weekly date nights with John to ensure we maintain us apart from business partners and parents.

I did achieve more Balance that year. I moved my health from the back burner to the top of my mind. I had a lot more fun with John, our kids, our friends, and in my business. I learned how to be of better service as a leader of a huge team, without making myself as stressed or crazy or exhausted . . . at least most of the time. Every time I strategized for my business, entertained an invitation or an opportunity, and made daily decisions on where to spend my time, I measured it against my Priorities and Goals. And if it didn't serve one of them, I didn't do it.

In the years since, my annual declarations and commitment to this process have made a huge difference in not only how much I've been able to accomplish in my personal and professional lives but also how much I've enjoyed the journey. In 2016, I declared my intention to *Grow* because I'd gotten too comfortable and found myself phoning it in all too often, scared to take things to the next level.

My Priorities in service of Grow were (again, in no particular order):

· I am healthy in mind, body, and soul.

· I create valuable ways to serve others by sharing my experience, inspiration, and coaching.

· I'm present in every moment and in all my relationships.

My Goals to serve my Priority of creating valuable ways to serve others included starting a new coaching program for our team that significantly contributed to a jaw-dropping number of success stories and 25 percent overall revenue growth that year. I also wrote my first book, allowing me to fulfill a lifelong dream and add bestselling author to wife, mom, and entrepreneur, and reach far more people than I could in my day-to-day business. To serve my Priority of being healthy in body, mind, and soul, I set a Goal of daily personal development reading to fill my head with positivity. And I committed to several workouts a week that reduced my stress and made me physically and mentally stronger, which helped me be more present in my life.

There were many other things that could've made my list of Priorities and Goals. But because I was laser-like Focused on this manageable blueprint I created, I stretched beyond where I thought possible in a year without being a raving lunatic.

So I hope you're getting the idea of how this works. Thousands of women have gone through this process with me over the years, and the One Words declared have been as diverse as the women themselves. Courage. Discipline. Intentional. Unstoppable. Flourish. Fierce. Sedulous (I had to look that one up; it means showing dedication and diligence). Rooted. Rocket. Moxie. I've loved how passionately they've publicly declared their intentions, even if they're not the type to make public declarations. "I did this for me, without thinking about what anyone else would think," said a team member through tears in a voice memo of thanks to me. "It makes me feel so much more powerful and hopeful than I did before you had me do this. Like I can really make things happen for me this year."

Now it's your turn to finish your One Word process so you know what to Focus on this year.

Take a moment and embrace your One Word again. Once you're all in with it and why, it's time to establish the two or three Priorities that serve your One Word. Remember, if they don't directly serve your One Word, while they may be worthwhile endeavors, they're not a Priority for you *right now*. As you figure out your top Priorities that serve your One Word, know that you may be putting some others on the back burner in exchange for the ones that are most important to you today. And that's OK. And then you set two or three Goals (remember, no more than five) that serve your Priorities.

I'm going to warn you: if you're anything like me and the tens of thousands of people I've walked through this process, once you start, you're going to hear your inner critic kick in. She will tell you that this is stupid or too hard to figure out, or that you can't possibly accomplish all this, or that some people important to you will think what you come up with is not what you should be focusing on. Acknowledge what your inner critic is saying, and then set it aside. As many wise people have said, you are not your thoughts or feelings.

I'm asking you to trust me and do the *entire* process. I've heard from enough people to know that the likelihood that you'll live in service to your One Word—that you'll grow in all parts of your life—is significantly reduced if you don't do the whole thing. Remember, simply declaring One Word, posting about it on Instagram and Facebook, and even sporting a hip metal washer bracelet isn't going to enhance or change your life. Like everything else that's worthwhile, it's going to take digging deep, doing the work, and being ruthlessly honest with yourself. So please do the work. If you do and get nothing out of it, you don't have to do it next year. But what if it transforms the way you think, work, play, love, and live? Would it be worth it?

It sure was for my team members Sarah Beyersdorf and Emily Paulson. Sarah and Emily followed this process with me in 2017, and what happened that year for both of them is nothing short of jaw-dropping.

SARAH

Sarah used to have a big corporate career in media sales but stepped away when she had her two kids. When her kids entered elementary school, she founded and ran a nonprofit that combines supporting women-owned businesses and impacting the lives of in-need families in her community. Then she started her own business to help fund her nonprofit. In 2016, that business quadrupled while Sarah juggled her kids, the responsibilities that came with often being a single parent while her husband, Kenny, traveled for his job, and a multitude of volunteer work. While on a family vacation in Southern California for the holidays, Sarah remembers wanting to celebrate everything in her life—her two kids' birthdays, earning a free car in her business, and getting to take a dream trip that included the Rose Bowl Parade—but she felt awful.

"My rheumatoid arthritis was horrible, I had gained all this weight, I was having chest pains from constant anxiety," Sarah remembers. "I had been so laser-focused on my business and the kids and my community work during the year, but I hadn't focused on me at all, and I was paying for it."

As 2017 started, Sarah chose *Decide* as her One Word, because she knew she had to decide what was really important to her and what she wanted her life to look like. "It became my mantra. Every day, all year long, I was constantly deciding whether every single thing that could take my time was serving my Priorities. And if it didn't, I didn't do it."

Sarah's first Priority was to live in vibrant health. That meant cutting out "the crap I was eating" on the go that was causing her arthritis to flare, instead making sure she took time for healthy meals. It also meant she had to rethink the way she rewarded herself. "My whole life I would celebrate an achievement with sweets or alcohol, but it was like poison to me."

Instead, Sarah started commemorating her goal-slaying with things that improved her health and gave her the quiet time her always-going brain needed, like yoga classes and massages. She lost forty-eight pounds, and her arthritis went into remission. "I had no pain in my feet for the first time in ten years!"

Her other Priorities were her family, with a Goal of being able to spend quality time with her kids every day, and running a huge business, with a Goal of reaching the top one percent of the field by September of that year. "If I was going to have time to do these things, I knew I had to stop being a control freak and admit I couldn't do it all myself."

Until then she had been doing everything for her nonprofit because she was "afraid to let anyone else touch my baby." When she hired an assistant to do all the time-consuming and tedious administrative work, she was able to Focus that time on growing her business. She also started to collaborate more, working with other teams to share coaching responsibilities and build a larger community of support and healthy competition. Sarah credits these changes with a huge spike in her productivity, which helped her reach her business goals four months early.

She also went to Kenny and admitted she needed help with the house and the kids now that she was running a big business alongside his crazy travel schedule. "He didn't know it was too much for me, because I hadn't told him," Sarah said. "But once I did, we started planning our lives like grown-ups." Kenny stepped up to share responsibilities when he was in town, they hired a housecleaner, and they hired a babysitter for when they'd both be out of town instead of Sarah trying to figure out which relative could take the kids.

"It turns out, I was a control freak," Sarah admitted. "Once I let go of trying to control everything, and admitted that I needed help, it was such a relief, and it made all the difference. It didn't make me weak; it made me human."

EMILY

Emily is a former chemist and science teacher who traded it all in to be a full-time mom to the five kids she had within seven years. I met her when she started her own business to take some of the financial burden off of her aerospace exec hubby, Kale, and enjoy more exposure to grown-ups. But I had no idea that behind the fast-growing entrepreneur was a cancer survivor with a serious drinking problem.

Emily had been in denial about her drinking for years, thinking that because she had stopped for periods of time—like when she was fighting cervical cancer—she wasn't an alcoholic. The beginning of her epiphany came on the very day that she earned a free car for her team's performance and ended up post-celebration in the back of a police car with a DUI. But it wasn't enough to get her to stop. She rationalized and played the part of a woman without a problem with great skill for six more months, even through court-ordered counseling and hospitalizations for alcohol toxicity symptoms.

Emily's last drink on New Year's Eve 2016 left her blacked out for an entire weekend. "I have no control," she remembers thinking. "I'm missing out on my life, my husband, and my kids, and I'm going to die." She started the year by joining Alcoholics Anonymous and diving into my One Word process, and she vowed to create a new *Vision* for what her life could be.

Emily's first Priority was that she and her family always come first. Her Goals of daily AA meetings, eating healthy, and getting enough sleep were nonnegotiable. So was being present for her family. For years she had been overwhelmed by the chaos of motherhood because "I thought I was supposed to be a perfect mom with a perfect family, and when life didn't look that way, I drank to escape." Once she decided to become part of the chaos and was OK with things like messes and piles of laundry and the noise, she no longer wanted to escape. Her Goals around her family were no longer about striving for perfection; they were about quality time together, including her now-favorite family activity: movie night on Fridays.

Another Priority was to honor her boundaries, which required her to let go of trying to be all things to all people—her husband, her kids, her kids' school, her team—and to say goodbye to people who didn't share her values. To serve these Priorities she established a nonnegotiable schedule that protected her time, which included working only with those in her business who actually wanted to work and making time only for those in her personal and professional lives with the same desire for success, health, and family.

By July, she had hit her business goals for the entire year, crediting her Focusing on the right things. Even more important, she became present in her life and learned why she had gotten to such a dark place.

She discovered that she had been self-medicating with alcohol instead of dealing with her feelings. "I always said I didn't care what other people thought," Emily said. "The truth is, I cared too deeply, and trying to be all things to all people was fueling my disease. When I focused on what I really wanted, what was really important to me, that's when I got healthy and felt like I was living my life, instead of trying to escape it."

YOUR PRIORITIES AND GOALS

OK, back to you. Write down your two or three Priorities and two or three Goals that serve each of them. And if you want more room, go to romineustadt.com/resources to download my One Word Process.

Priority: ....

    Goals: 1. ....

          2. ....

          3. ....

Priority: ....

    Goals: 1. ....

          2. ....

          3. ....

Priority: ....

    Goals: 1. ....

          2. ....

          3. ....

Now that you've established your Priorities and set your Goals, you know what to Focus on. So you and I are done, right? Not so fast. I've learned from experience that it's not quite that easy. Even the most intense soul-searching—whether in a Four Seasons suite or your local Starbucks—that results in the most carefully crafted trinity of your One Word, Priorities, and Goals won't get you living your best life or being the human you were designed and destined to be without figuring some other things out.

Because you're dealing with all the things that got you to pick up this book in the first place. Remember, we already covered this: you've grown up, and your life has gotten cluttered with the Shoulds, the internal and the external voices, the endless to-do lists, and how success oftentimes begets more Shoulds and voices and to-do lists. And then an entire year has passed and you've not only *not* been able to Focus on the things you really wanted to, you've exhausted your body, mind, and spirit with everything else and are feeling like a lost soul and a failure.

So now that you know *what* you want to Focus on, the most important thing for you to do is figure out all the things you *won't* be focusing on. And I know it's going to be hard for you to let go of some of them. Trust me, I get it. But I'll be right here with you, explaining why it's so important to **Focus on Less**, so you can **Live More and Be More**. And once we've cleared a lot off your plate and out of your brain, we're going to Focus you on the most important things, not just this year but every year.

If that makes you take a deep breath of relief followed by an exhale of faith, good girl. Because you've got this. There are plenty more tools I'm going to lay at your feet to show you that you have plenty of time and that there's plenty of you for the stuff that's really important to you.

Three

KNOW WHAT YOUR
TIME IS WORTH

Know your worth, and then add tax.

—Anonymous

Y ou've likely heard countless times that our most valuable resource is time. The older I get and the faster life whizzes by, the more I cling to this truth. But how valuable? It dawned on me years ago that if I figured out the monetary value of my time, I'd be more likely to make smart decisions about where I spent it. I was great at not buying a new handbag every month, but I gave out thirty-minute "let me pick your brain" sessions to anyone who could find my email address—even though six times out of seven the answers to all their questions were easily accessed elsewhere, like the company's backend library or Google. I was careful about not wasting hundreds of dollars, but I was too cavalier about wasting my time or spending it on the wrong things. So I came up with a way to figure out my hourly worth, which gave me the mathematical proof I needed to make it a no-brainer to stop doing some things and delegate others. And by the time you're done with this chapter, you're going to have the mathematical proof to know *your* hourly worth, and you'll also see—in black and white or whatever color pen you use—that your wasted time is wasted money.

In the next chapter I'm going to be talking to you about all the things you need to stop doing. I'm not going to sugarcoat it: it's going to be really hard for you to swallow because you're a woman, and most of us have a genetic predisposition to think we can and should be doing everything for everyone. And that asking for help is a weakness.

But once we understand what our time is worth, it's a hell of a lot easier to let go of the habits, tasks, thoughts, and other various BS that aren't serving our Priorities or helping us reach our Goals. And I promise you, your time is worth *a lot* more than you think.

YOUR DREAM LIFE

First, you've got to figure out the life you want. Maybe you're living it, although I doubt it, since you bought this book. Take a few minutes and get really clear on what you want your life to look like in the next five years. I want you to answer the following questions in the space provided (or grab a journal if you need more room). Here's the rule: you're not allowed to censor your vision with doubts or negative voices or by replaying past failures. Shut off any internal discussion of what's practical or doable and allow yourself to dream about what you really want.

1. Where do you live? What does your home look like?

....

....

2. What does your family look like? Spouse or partner, kids, pets?

....

....

3. If you have kids, where do they go to school? What activities are they involved in?

....

....

4. What are you doing professionally? Is it different from what you're doing now?

....

....

5. If you have a spouse or partner, what is he or she doing professionally, and is it different from what he or she is doing now?

....

....

6. Do you travel, and if so, how often and to where?

....

....

7. Do you have any debt?

....

....

8. Do you have a savings account you can easily access
   in case the shit hits the fan, and how many months of
   living expenses are in there?

....

....

9. Do you contribute to a retirement fund and/or a college fund?

....

....

10. What else do you love about your future life?

....

....

This is your vision of what you really want, what it will look
like for you to Have It All.

So what's this life going to cost you? How much do you need
to earn a year to live this dream?

My dream life costs $_____ per year.

Let's stop right here for a second. I talk about money a lot in
my business because I help people earn more of it. But discussing

what you earn, or what you want to earn, may make you uncomfortable. I get that. I'm not suggesting that money is a measure of self-worth. Money simply gives us more options. What I want you to get real about is how much money you want to make to have the life you want to live.

For many of you, you're likely not earning what you need to live your dream life. Unless you're planning on winning the lottery, it's going to require you to do something to bring in more income. You may be able to increase your earnings enough through your current profession by putting in more time and effort. For example, if you're a lawyer and your dream life can be achieved with partner-level income, then you'll probably need to bill more hours and do what it takes to bring in business to make yourself stand out to the selection committee. If you're a teacher, but you want to transition to a role in education administration, you may need an advanced degree or to take on additional responsibilities to gain the required experience.

If your dream life can't be funded by your current profession, you're not alone. This is one of the primary reasons why so many people have side hustles to provide additional income and explore passions without interfering with their day jobs, or to build an escape ramp from their existing jobs. A 2018 Bankrate survey found that nearly four in ten (37 percent) of Americans have a side job. If you're a headhunter, maybe you'll decide you can create a consulting business on the side to teach people how to make their résumés and interview performance more effective. If you're part of an in-house marketing department, maybe you'll pick up freelance work. If you're a photographer who works for a newspaper, you might create a side biz doing family photo shoots. The best waitress at one of our favorite restaurants has a full-time job she loves in an architecture firm, but she also loves the tips she earns that fund her world travels.

For more than a decade, I've been helping people create new streams of income to supplement or completely replace their existing incomes, depending on their goals. So I know with 100 percent certainty that if you need to bring in more income to live your dream life, it's going to require more of your time. The trick is to find the extra time.

When the company I work with fell into my lap, I had already figured out what my five-years-out dream life looked like. I had done enough personal development work to know that if I didn't get clear about where I wanted to go, I'd never get there. I just didn't know how the hell I was going to get there.

My dream included owning my own schedule, affording anything my kids wanted to pursue, contributing toward flush retirement accounts that would give John and me more options, and feeding the kids' college funds at a rate that would fully pay for whatever school they chose. John and I knew this life would require hundreds of thousands of dollars of additional income a year. While he was building his side hustle around his medical practice—his dietary supplement business—we had no idea when or if it was going to be a large income generator. So I had to figure out how to increase my income, and it wasn't going to be through PR if I ever wanted to see our kids.

You've already heard how full my plate was when I started my business, and adding an entrepreneurial venture didn't give me more time; it required more of my time. If I was going to be able to build this sucker and stay sane, I had to start viewing my time as a commodity to help me make better decisions about where to spend it.

Because I'm a doer, I knew that I needed a way to screen where my time was going to go and an excuse to redline the things I'd have a tendency to pile on my plate that shouldn't be there. I needed to figure out what my time was worth. Since I'd previously worked in professions ruled by the billable hour (law and public relations), I wanted to figure out what my time was worth—my billable hour, if you will—based on what I wanted to earn. So I came up with a mathematical formula to figure it out. And trust me when I say math is not my strong suit, so this was a really big deal.

It required me to first decide on two numbers:

1. **How much did I want to earn annually?** To really understand the value of my time, I knew I couldn't limit myself to what I would be bringing in next month or next year. I had to come up with the *big* number. I wasn't an expert yet on building my business back then, but I knew enough to know that if I wanted to build a life-changing business, I had to value my time, not according to the now but according to the future I wanted.

2. **How many hours a week did I want to work?** If I was really going to design a life where I owned my time, part of figuring out what my time was worth also had to include how many hours a week I ultimately wanted to work. Not the number of hours I thought I'd have to work to reach my *big* number, but how many hours I wanted to be working every week on income-producing endeavors once I hit that number.

I came up with an incredibly audacious goal—to earn one million dollars a year. And even if I didn't reach it, what's the worst that could happen? I shoot for the moon and land among the stars, somewhere in the extra few hundred grand a year. I knew it wouldn't happen overnight and that it would take a tremendous amount of work, but I also knew that it would help me ensure I never had to work for anyone else ever again and could forever own my time. "Why not me?" I thought.

As for my second number, I decided I wanted to be working my business twenty hours a week. That would give me plenty of time to be a hands-on mom, get workouts in, spend time with John, and still have some left over to devote to causes I care about. All the stuff that was in my dream life. Please note, I had no illusions that I'd be working twenty hours a week while I was building to those earnings. It was my goal I was working toward.

Here are my calculations from back then:

20 hours per week × 52 weeks = 1,040 hours per year

$1 million ÷ 1,040 hours per year = $962 per hour

Every hour of my time was worth $962! That blew my mind and my billable rate as a lawyer or PR consultant out of the water. Do you think that had an impact on how I spent my time? You better believe it did!

When someone on my team wanted to take part of my day to blame her lack of success on external factors for the fifth time, I was not about to flush $240 down the toilet for that fifteen-minute phone call. I knew that every hour I spent watching TV or mindlessly scrolling on social media was $962 down the toilet. Must-see TV didn't seem quite so important. And if I could pay a college student twelve dollars an hour to fold laundry and clean up the kids' toys so I could use that time to build my business, that's a financial no-brainer.

As my goals have changed—how much I want to earn and how many hours I want to work—I've consistently recalculated as my income has blown past my audacious goal. At any given time I'm crystal clear on my time's hourly worth. It helps me continue to refine where I spend my time and where I don't. As I write this, every hour of my time is worth $9,615. Is that my reality right now? Nope. But it's what I'm working toward.

Now it's your turn to calculate your time's hourly worth. But before you do, we need to have a little talk. Because I bet you may have a voice inside your head, telling you you're not worthy of a *big* number of your own. Don't feel badly; you're not alone. I've taken thousands of people through this exercise, and with few exceptions, women lowball themselves. And when I call them on it, if we're face-to-face in the real world or via video conference, I can literally watch them shrink back into a shrug of resignation that says, "How dare I even shoot for that much, let alone what I really want?"

Here's the thing: you're worthy of whatever you're willing to work your ass off to achieve. Period. You need to dream *big* about what your determination, grit, consistency, and daily efforts can lead you to, because it will keep you from wasting your time on the activities, emotions, and people that aren't serving your Priorities and Goals.

And *big* is unique to each of us. Your dream life may not require an income anywhere close to mine. This is your life, your dreams, so all I'm asking is that you be honest with yourself and not give the naysaying voices in your head any power.

The women I coach have told me this process is life-changing, so get to it.

_____ hours per week × 52 weeks = _____ hours per year

_____ ÷ _____ = $ _____ per hour
(annual income)   (hours/year)

My Time Is Worth $_____ per Hour!

Before we move on, go back to your number and make sure you haven't lowballed your dreams. Repeat after me: "I'm worthy." If you need to go back and recalculate, do it. I'll wait; I'm not going anywhere.

OK, now that you have your number, I hope you're thinking, "Wow, I'm the shit." Because you are. Or shit-in-the-making. Either way, you now have undeniable proof how inefficient, financially irresponsible, and downright crazy it is for you to spend time doing things that don't serve your Priorities or help you achieve your Goals. Or to keep doing things when it makes financial sense for you to pay someone else to do it. Or to waste time on people and emotions that don't serve you.

Now that you know what your time is worth, I get to help you figure out all the things you're going to stop doing. Watch out, Marie Kondo. We're about to spark some serious joy.

Four

RELENTLESSLY EDIT
YOUR LIFE

Keep only those things that speak to your heart.
Then take the plunge and discard all the rest.

—Marie Kondo

I know that at different parts of your life (like maybe this
morning) you've said out loud, muttered under your breath,
or exclaimed through sobs, "There's just not enough time!" I
know I have.

Now that you know what every single hour of your life is worth,
it's going to be much easier for you to swallow this process
I'm about to take you through to relentlessly edit your life. By the
time you finish this chapter, you're going to have a thorough
understanding of where you're putting your time and why, and
what things you're going to stop doing either by deleting them

completely or delegating them to someone else because their hourly rate is lower than your hourly worth.

Remember, the point is to Have It All, *not* Do It All.

ARE YOU PRODUCTIVE OR JUST BUSY?

Let's all be honest here: we're confusing being productive with being busy. I've learned that the really great stuff in life—the true growth and breakthroughs—come after periods of time when we're productive. Consistently working on what's going to get us to where we want to be. Instead, too many of us are focused on being busy. And people who are busy often are the least productive.

How many times has someone asked you, "How are you?" or "What's going on in your life?" and you've answered, "I'm so busy!"

The logical next question they ask is, "What are you so busy with?" And you pause and think for a minute, and then respond with a laundry list of the tasks on any given day's to-do list. Or maybe you offer up an exhausted, "Oh, you know, *life*."

I'm not judging, truly. I've given those responses. Many, many times. Before and after I was a mom, a super-successful entrepreneur, and an author. And every time I offered up a similar response, I'd feel even more overwhelmed and exhausted and disappointed in myself. Because deep down, I knew that all the stuff that was eating up my time—that I was *allowing* to eat up my time—wasn't what I really wanted to be doing. And I longed to be able to answer with passion and purpose about things that were really filling my soul.

What if your answer was an energetic, powerful sharing of

your Priorities or your top Goals that you're currently working toward? If that's where all your time was going, those are the things that would be on the top of your mind and the tip of your tongue. How would that feel? What if all of us were walking around having conversations about our Priorities and Goals, supporting and cheering on one another, instead of lamenting how busy we were and how little time we had to get it *All* done? We women are spending our time on the wrong All. Imagine what we could do and who we could become if we were clearing out all the crap that isn't serving us and focusing only on the stuff that's important to us.

WHERE DOES YOUR TIME GO?

So let's figure out how much of your time you're spending on the wrong All. I'm going to take you through an exercise I do at least twice a year, and I've coached my team to do it too. This two-step exercise is going to show you exactly where all your time is going. If you half-ass it, it's not going to give you the information you need about where you're spending your time and you might as well not bother. So go *All In*.

1. I want you to write down everything you do over the course of a week in all parts of your life, and how long you spend on it. And I mean everything. Grab a notebook and carry it with you everywhere, or download my Edit Your Life Log at romineustadt.com/resources, so you can capture Every. Single. Thing. you do for seven days. Just like an eating log if you're trying to figure out what you're putting in your pie hole, if you don't write

down everything you're spending your time on, it's not going to help you identify what you need to change.

2. Once you've spent a whole week recording your life, look at everything listed on every day and categorize each entry.

- Mark "P" for everything that serves one or more of your Priorities.

- Mark "G" for everything that's helping you get closer to achieving one or more of your Goals.

- Mark "F" for everything that's just plain Fun.

- Mark "H" for everything you Hate doing.

- Mark "S" for everything you think you Should Do.

- Mark "M" for everything you think you Must Do.

As you label each activity, really think about how it should be categorized, and call BS on yourself if you need to. The things that are marked "P" and "G" are what you should be doing, if in fact they truly serve your Priorities and Goals. And the things you're doing for "F"un? Girls gotta have fun, so you get to keep those, too. Plus, if you did serious soul searching in the One Word process, the Fun things you're doing will likely be serving at least one of your Priorities and Goals.

Those you mark "M" must truly be the things you cannot possibly avoid, like sleeping, basic hygiene (showering, brushing and flossing your teeth, etc.), taking time to fuel your body, and going to the bathroom. (Hey, I told you to write down everything.) Anything else doesn't get an "M."

The entries you've marked "H" or "S" or those without a label because you can't figure out what they are? That's where we're going to spend our time together. If I could, I would grab your time log, shine a light on each of those entries, and cue a chorus to start singing, "Hallelujah, hallelujah, hallelu-u-u-jah!" Because I get to help you take a critical look at them, and by the time we're done, I'm certain you'll be able to exchange these tasks for more time for your Priorities, your Goals, and your sanity.

HATES AND SHOULDS

I want us to focus on the items on your Hate and Should lists. I have a pretty good idea what's on there because you're probably like me and the women I've coached: housecleaning, laundry, administrative work in your professional and personal lives, finances, cooking dinner, grocery shopping, volunteering for the school book drive, baking from scratch, handmaking Valentine's, and more. Oh, so much more.

There's an undeniable truth for the modern woman that's reached an epidemic proportion: we're Should-ing all over the place. The problem with Shoulds is that they don't support our Priorities or help us reach our Goals. And often, we're doing the things we Hate to do because we think we Should. Should happens because of real or made-up societal pressure. Because of the BS we're telling ourselves. And we need to stop.

Repeat after me: *I cannot do everything.* Really, say it. And here's another one: *I'm not supposed to be able to do everything.*

How good does that feel? Pretty damn good, because at the root of us doing all these Shoulds is our belief that we're supposed to do everything, and if we're unable to, there's something wrong with us.

I recognized early on in my entrepreneurial career that if I was going to be one of those seven-figure CEOs that I aspired to be, I wouldn't be able to do everything. And here's the greatest part: I didn't *have* to. In fact, doing the things I Hated or thought I Should not only took my time away from the things I really wanted to do, but they also zapped my energy and made me less productive in all parts of my life. And I would routinely procrastinate those things anyway, which left me feeling guilty or like a failure and really screwed up my ability to get to my Priorities.

BECOME A MASTER DELEGATOR

Delegating is not a weakness; it's a superpower. And we've all got to get comfortable doing it if we want to Have It All. I remembered what a former PR client of mine had told me years before I started a family. I was driving Nell Merlino, the founder of Take Our Daughters and Sons to Work Day (originally called Take Our Daughters to Work Day), to a press event for her new venture, Count Me In, which is still thriving in its promotion of economic independence for women and the growth of women-owned businesses. She said, "You know the reason there aren't more women millionaires, Romi? Women don't delegate. They don't know how to or they refuse to learn. And it's costing them dearly."

I vowed right then, that as my professional life grew, I would delegate everything I could in all parts of my life. And I learned through the years that it's just as important to delete everything we can from our full plates. So when I started growing my own business, I started to carefully analyze what I was doing with my time. And anything that could free up my time to do the things I really wanted to do was fair game for the chopping block, either by delegating or deleting.

I want to make something clear: you don't have to be a business owner or have aspirations of six- or seven-figure earnings in order to employ the magic of delegating and deleting. You just have to be a human who wants to live a more intentional and fulfilling life.

It costs money to delegate and delete. So your knee-jerk reaction (and perhaps your spouse's or life partner's) might be that you Shouldn't spend the money. You might be telling yourself that since you're not making a certain amount of money, you Should be doing everything yourself. But remember your hourly worth? If you can pay someone else to do things for you and it costs less than your hourly worth, then it not only makes financial sense, I argue it's actually an essential business expense. An essential *life* expense. Because it will free you up to Focus on what's really important to you.

I don't understand people who will buy things instead of buying more services that will save them time and make them healthier. And I see it all the time. I'll be coaching people about this very topic, and they'll tell me there's no way they can afford it. And a few days later I'll see them post about their new Louis Vuitton bag that sure as hell isn't going to remove anything from their to-do list or reduce their stress.

So here's the question I started asking myself about everything I was doing, and it's the question you should constantly be asking yourself too: *Is there someone else who can do this, or am I the only person uniquely qualified?*

When I was in start-up mode for my business with a baby and

a preschooler, there was no way I could wear all the hats that wanted space on my head. One of those hats was Chef of the House. I've always loved cooking, and until I started my own business, I was the cook. It was clear, however, that this chef needed to be chopped from the meals schedule during the week so I could have more time to focus on growing my business. John started adding to his culinary repertoire beyond the infamous "pepper chicken" from early in our marriage (yes, it was just chicken and pepper, God love him). But he was in start-up mode for his business, along with his medical practice, so cooking once a week was all he could fit in. I dropped any guilt I felt—and any feelings that I Should be cooking more along with it—and embraced healthy meal assembly and the virtues of takeout. This was before the plethora of meals-in-a-box options and meal delivery options that are available now, which my start-up self would've had an orgasm over. I also made the most out of cooking one afternoon a week for that night's dinner and to stock the freezer, while also catching up on the recorded calls that were a foundation of the training back then in the company I work with.

Contrast this with a member of my team a few years ago who said she wanted to build her own business and say goodbye to a full-time job that wasn't allowing her to live the life she envisioned. Yet she couldn't find time in her evenings to work her side gig because she said she had to make a "home-cooked meal from scratch" for her family every night. That was a Priority, but building a life-changing business was not. Or else it was a Should she was telling herself, and she was unwilling to explore why she was putting this pressure on herself so she could let it go. If cooking every night was her Priority, I don't judge her for that. But I had to make it clear to her—and now to you—that we can't do everything. And if our Priorities are at odds with each other, we're going to have to make a choice. The choice that's right for us.

It also made no sense to me back then to spend my valuable time cleaning the house when we could pay someone else twenty dollars an hour to do it. I wasn't a big-time success when we hired our first cleaning lady to come to us twice a month. But I considered it a business expense. Our first few didn't do our laundry, and while I had no problem throwing loads into the washer and dryer, I sure hated folding it and still do. So I paid our babysitters extra to fold our laundry and keep the kids' clothes organized, and was it worth it. Now with the Marie Kondo craze, if you #konmari your closet and drawers, your laundry helper can help you and hone her tidying skills and get social media fodder while she's at it. This will #sparkjoy for everyone.

After I figured out how much time I was spending every month to pay our bills and manage our expenses, we hired a bookkeeper to do it, making it super easy for our accountant to file our taxes. Both were definitely worth more than their professional fees because their hourly fees were considerably less than my hourly worth. Plus the time it freed up for John and me, not to mention dramatically reducing the possibility of costly errors on our part because we're far from experts, was invaluable. Unless the finances in your life or business are so complex or labor-intensive, a bookkeeper is likely unnecessary now, thanks to technology and the abundance of autopay options and apps to help you track expenses and receipts to make the most of deductions come tax time. But I wanted you to understand the thought process John and I went through to make these delegating decisions, so you can apply it to all parts of your life.

Examine everything you're doing in your work—whether you're

in real estate, insurance, law, sales, interior design, you name it. If there are things that you suck at or don't want to do that you can pay someone else to do for less than your hourly worth, do it. If you want to ramp up your social media presence but don't know how or don't want to make eye-catching shareables to go along with the content that you want to put out there, pay someone else to make them. I even have team members whose high school– and college-age kids do this for them for spending money and a great line item on their résumés. Absolutely hate social media? There are people who will do it all for you if you supply them with your authentic voice and content nuggets. And it will cost you a hell of a lot less than what it costs you to spin your wheels or drag yourself for hours and hours through something that you Hate.

In my profession, the ways to serve our customers and our team members grow along with our businesses. I always coach those I mentor to get help as soon as possible so they can delegate tasks that someone else can do, to free them up to do more of the parts of the business only they can do. These tasks can include keeping track of all our team members who earn trips or cars with our company so we can give them much-deserved recognition, project-managing holiday cards, packing and addressing mail, making trips to the post office, and running other errands. Admittedly, many of the entrepreneurs I work with actually like this stuff and find it easier than doing the hard part of our gig— putting themselves out there to talk to people. But I tell them that as soon as their hourly worth surpasses the hourly rate of an assistant, they must stop doing this stuff if they want to grow large, life-changing businesses.

If you're like me and have control-freak tendencies, you may think that no one can do things as well as you can, or it will be too hard to teach someone, so you Should keep doing them. Since I've been there and proven both of these assertions to be flawed, I'm calling bullshit on you. You may be right that no one can do a particular task as well as you can, but that's not the analysis, remember? It's this: *Is there someone else who can do this, or am I the only person uniquely qualified?* And who knows, you may be surprised like I have been when the person you've hired to do things you're fabulous at ends up becoming even better at them than you are.

If you're concerned about the time and effort it takes to teach someone your way of doing things in the short term, add up all the hours it's going to take you to continue to do those things in the long term. How much is that going to cost you, Ms. Control Freak?

And let's be honest here about this whole control-freak concept. It should really be called an out-of-control freak. Those of us who have dealt with this tendency, or condition, or whatever you want to call it, are afraid of letting go because of what will happen. Guess what? We don't have total control over everything we keep on our plates either. But what we do have control over is the calculation of our hourly worth and deciding what makes financial sense to delegate.

As your income grows because you have more time to further your career, reinvest some of the increase back into your business by constantly reviewing what you can pay someone else to do in all parts of your life. I'm routinely taking a look at all the things I don't want to do or calling BS on the things I think I Should be doing—and so do John and I as a couple—and I delegate it or delete it. All. Of. It.

I know for a fact that my business couldn't have grown as meteorically fast in those first few years—while still keeping my health and marriage intact—without the amazing Krista Seneker handling everything I lobbed onto her court for both my business and my personal lives. And for the last several years, it's been a combo of Ianthe Andress, my virtual assistant extraordinaire in Washington State (whom I've never actually met in person) and Linda Branson, who John and I joke is our wife, and who the kids call Mrs. B. She's evolved over the years from part childcare giver and part assistant to how we affectionately now refer to her, COO of our household and a member of our family. I get to delegate every single thing Linda can do to help me in my roles of mom, entrepreneur, pet owner, and home owner. As I wrote in the acknowledgments of my first book, Linda fills in "all the spaces I leave (and there are many) and made it possible for me to have writing time without the wheels coming off the bus. You also make it possible for John and me to fly off to be badass biz builders, or just have some peace and quiet and get some."

Admittedly, some of the things Linda does might be the very things that serve your Priorities and Goals, and you have no desire to delegate them—nor should you. But I want to be transparent for everyone out there who has dreams of juggling family and a thriving, evolving professional life and self-care. I'm able to Have It All because I'm not Doing It All. Linda is a necessary expense because she enables me to do what I do and live the kind of life I want to live. And once she reads this, I'm fully prepared for a compensation adjustment conversation.

DO YOU REALLY HATE IT?

Remember, often we're doing the things we Hate to do because we think we Should. Take exercise, for example. Maybe you marked working out as Hate, but one of your Priorities is to "Live with a healthy mind and body." You know that one of the keys to a healthy bod is moving it. Maybe you Hate it because you haven't yet found the kind of exercise you like in an environment that's comfortable, head-clearing, energizing. Maybe you've been thinking you Should be a part of this Orangetheory or CrossFit craze because a lot of your friends are having great success and fun with it. But it's too similar to the regimented, fast pace of your day job, where you're constantly measured by time and how much you can produce in that time. Instead of leaving you feeling recharged, empowered, and working toward your overall wellness, it gives you a headache and a big case of the inadequacies.

You're not the problem; it's simply that this type of exercise isn't the right fit for you. As my life got busier and fuller—with work, growing kids, more people wanting my time, more stimulus coming at me—the types of workouts I used to pursue were no longer what I needed. It took me years to realize that I was choosing Tabata classes and kickboxing and hard-core circuit training because of Shoulds and BS I was telling myself, and it was fracturing my lifelong love affair with physical activity.

"Hard-core, hard-driving workouts are the way for me to be sculpted and thin," I was still telling myself, "and I should be as sculpted and thin as I possibly can be. And I'm a driven, competitive person, so the push-push-push of these workouts is perfect for my personality, and that's the kind of exercise I should be doing. And these are the kinds of workouts I did in my twenties and thirties, and if I no longer want to do them, it means I'm—gasp—getting old."

Here's what I realized after years of declining passion for my workouts and waning consistency from this otherwise incredibly consistent chick: my workouts weren't serving my Priorities and Goals. My idea of health and wellness had evolved from wanting to be as thin and sculpted as possible to wanting to be as healthy and strong as possible. And my sacred workout time was as much about clearing my head and recharging my energy as it was about taking care of my body.

I had to silence the voices in my head that were telling me what I Should be doing. I'm really happy for those folks in the CrossFit and Orangetheory social media posts I see, and I'm cheering them on, truly. But I'm now obsessed with yoga—power and hatha— and also love long walks with hill intervals and a great podcast, and functional workouts that are gentler on my body and my mind. This is what I need to serve my Priorities and Goals in my life right now. And wouldn't you know, my bod is responding in a way I haven't seen since long before I started popping out kids, and I actually look forward to and love my workout time.

MOM GUILT IS THE BIGGEST PILE OF SHOULDS OUT THERE

Us moms are loving and supporting and kind to our offspring, but we're wicked good at being ruthlessly tough on ourselves. As if there's a manual out there somewhere that lays out everything moms are supposed to do and be, and when we compare ourselves, we fall way short.

Sure, there are moms out there who come pretty close to the description in the aforementioned manual: those who remember to turn in every permission slip and volunteer for class mom and host the end-of-year party and be the backstage mom at the dance recital and and and. I applaud them. But here's what I believe to my core: being a great mom isn't about living up to an unrealistic job description, no matter what Pinterest or Instagram or that annoying, critical voice in our heads tells us.

Thankfully, it didn't take me long into my motherhood journey to realize that if I was going to be the kind of mom my kids deserved (loving, fulfilled, without resentment, healthy, present when I really needed to be), I had to Focus on the parts of the job that I was uniquely qualified to do.

Those parts didn't and still don't include a lot of things other moms might do. Like crafts. Because I jokingly refer to myself as the Martha Stewart anti-Christ, I've always marveled at the crafty moms, like the one who would hand-sew her child's Valentines every year. But I don't enjoy that stuff, except for the occasional school project. (I'm quite proud of my collaboration with Nate on an adorable little Russian Jew circa 1880 we made out of felt and googly eyes for Heritage Week. Bebe's little babushka when it was her turn was pretty cute too.) And I don't apologize for it. The kids get their craft fix elsewhere, and they know it's not my jam. It's even a family joke, and I always laugh the hardest.

Although I found it pretty simple to quiet my internal voices of what I should be doing as a mom, it wasn't quite as easy for me when the Mom Guilt came from outside critics. When we moved to San Diego and to our kids' first elementary school, as a working mom I found myself in the minority. I was still in the hyper-building part of my business and wasn't super-active leading committees or serving as class mom or on the PTA. But I did what was expected of parents to contribute to the community. What sucked was when I was judged for contributing in a way that was less than what other moms deemed acceptable.

Like when I brought my store-bought offering for the cake-walk fundraiser at the school carnival. I'll never forget walking into the classroom that was serving as the cake storage unit, with a rainbow of home-baked, Food Network–worthy offerings covering the desks. It was like a scene out of the movie *Bad Moms*, as one of the organizers greeted me with a smile, which faded once she looked down at my obvious grocery store effort, complete with a Ralphs sticker on it.

"Oh, you *bought* it?" she said as a question when we both knew it was a factual statement. I thanked her for all her hard work to make the event a success, which was met with a curt "Oh, it's nothing," and a quick turn on her heel into the sea of cakes to put mine in the back. The way back.

Fuck you very much, Ms. Eye-Roll-with-the-Perfect-Pony-and-the-Chic-Lululemons. Baking a cake that week—or any week that isn't my kid's birthday—doesn't serve my Priorities, and if you wanted "from scratch," the two hundred emails and flyers the kids brought home should've said that. Of course I didn't say that to her, but it's sure what I was muttering to myself on the way home.

Later that night, when I was still miffed, I dug deep and asked myself why. It wasn't because of me and my choices; I sure as hell wasn't second-guessing them. It was about what *she thought* about me and my choices. Why did I care? Because I'm human. But once I identified that I was bothered because of external judgment and not because of what I considered important for me, it was easy for me to find comfort and return to confidence.

Then there was the time the snarky dance mom commented that I didn't know about a rehearsal time change because "You never do drop off, and we never see you around for Bebe." It was the *"for Bebe"* that was the obvious dig. This time I didn't care. It was a few years after the cake incident, and I was more confident, more comfortable in my own skin, even more successful and increasingly more satisfied with my life and the choices that made my life possible. True, I drove and still do drive the kids to fewer than half of their extracurricular activities because I can be far more productive during those pockets when they aren't talkative or need to wolf down a snack or do homework during the drive time. And getting other things done during that time leaves more time for me to be with the kids when I can make a real impact, like helping with homework, helping them prep for auditions, listening to them talk about their latest challenge or disappointment or dream, teaching them time management skills, or doing the other gazillion things that go along with kids who are involved in the arts. Or sports. Or whatever it is that your kid is into.

I didn't get miffed at Dance Mom. I smiled and laughed and then marched over to the studio owner to kindly ask her to email all relevant time changes moving forward. And instead of muttering to myself on the way home, I turned on CNN.

I'm raising kids who know what I am and what I'm not, and not being able to—or choosing not to—do everything that a mom can possibly do has enabled me to build a fulfilling and lucrative career that makes their life pretty damn incredible. It also allows me to take care of myself so that they're getting the best of me for—please, God—a really long time. Long enough to be an amazing grandmother. Who might even do crafts with her grandkids.

I posted an image on social media during the busy holiday season last year that read, "Moms, instead of judging each other, let's support each other like we used to when we were single and drunk in club bathrooms." My accompanying post read, "I know it's the holidays and it's crazy busy and we're all stretched in so many ways and running on less sleep than normal. But let's remember, we're all on the same team. #peaceonearth."

It's one of my most popular posts of all time because we're all feeling judged, by ourselves and by one another. Neither you nor I can control the thoughts and actions of Ms. Eye Roll in her Lulus. And let's face it, there will always be someone with an eye roll or a snarky comment. But for the love of God, let's make sure it's not us—whether we're talking to another mom or to ourselves.

So, how many things have you marked H or S that you're doing because you think it's what a good mom Should do? Hopefully you'll start to treat yourself as kindly as you treat your kids and you'll stop that shit.

A FEW WORDS ABOUT SCREENS

I'm going to talk more about social media later, but I've got to spend a few minutes on it now. When you captured everything you did during the week, I'm pretty sure you logged time spent on social media. It's quite likely that some of that time was to serve your Priorities and Goals because you use it in your work, your volunteer efforts, or even some aspects of parenting. In my business, social media is a powerful tool in our toolkit, and as a writer and speaker, I use social to promote my books, blogs, and appearances.

Yet even though you may have marked your social media time with a P or G, you've got to make sure that every minute you logged was actually in furtherance of your Ps and Gs. I know from personal experience and from coaching tens of thousands who have to be on social just how easy it is to get sidetracked from what you went on there to do in the first place.

It's also quite likely that you have social media time logged as F, because most of us use Facebook or Instagram or Snapchat or the other app du jour for entertainment. If you were accurately capturing all your time, many of you found that you spend a lot of time endlessly scrolling through social in the name of Fun or relaxation. Perhaps you should change the label to an A for Addiction. I'm not being judgy like Eye Roll Mom, because I've been there too. Cognitive neuroscientists have shown that rewarding social stimuli—such as a "like" on Instagram or a Facebook notification—can give our brains a hit of dopamine and leave us wanting more and more and more. This is like the response our brains get to drugs and refined sugar. And breaking the time-sucking addiction to our phones and social media can be particularly hard for those of us who use these platforms for our work. I'm living proof that it's possible to stay away from refined sugar, but I have to be on my phone, iPad, and social media nearly every day. We can acknowledge if we have a problem, label that time accurately, and then hang on until chapter 6, when I'll help you break your addiction with healthy social media habits.

Now let's talk TV, Netflix binge-watching, YouTube video wormholes, and the like. You probably have some or a lot of this on your list with an F next to it. And that's great. But if you're complaining that you don't have enough time to get to the stuff that's serving your Priorities and Goals, some of that screen time has got to go. For the first five years of my business, unless I was on a piece of cardio equipment or it was Oscars night, I didn't watch TV. I still don't watch all the TV that looks interesting because there are so many other things I want to do, and because I really do try to parent by example. I'm not letting myself start the new season of *The Marvelous Mrs. Maisel* until this book is done because I'm only so strong. And once this cake is baked, I'll do a couple of weekends of bingeing, if and only if there's nothing else more Fun for me to be doing in the real world. Because the truth is, Mrs. Maisel will still be there next year. And the year after. But I'd sure hate to delay achieving my Goals because of her.

If you're spending time on screens for relaxation instead of spending time moving forward on the parts of your life you've identified as important, it's quite likely you're feeling stressed and out of balance because of all the entries you marked H or S. When you delete or delegate those and free up time for your Ps and Gs, I bet you'll find that you don't crave as much screen time. Crazy how that works, isn't it?

SAYING NO

By now, I hope you'll agree with me that the number one reason most of us aren't getting to the things that are really important to us is because we don't know how to say **No**. To ourselves, to others, to societal pressures (or perceived societal pressures). Why is this itty-bitty word so damn hard for us? Because deep down in our female souls, we want to be liked (and loved), and we're afraid that saying No will make people not like or love us. If we don't do what others expect or want from us (or what we've allowed ourselves to believe is expected or wanted of us), we've somehow lost self-worth.

We've been talking a lot about saying No to ourselves and unrealistic expectations, and yes to deleting and delegating. While it's one thing to say No to yourself and strike something off your own to-do list, it's quite another to say it out loud to other people to decline invitations and requests for your time. But if you don't get really comfortable saying it, your One Word will be irrelevant because you'll never get to it and everything that flows from it. Fuhgeddaboudit.

When I first started my business, I had to say No a lot. No, I can't take on extra clients just because you really want my expertise. No, I won't be able to teach Hebrew school this year. No, I can't head up the Montessori fundraiser. No, I can't have sex with you tonight because, I promise you, it will be like doing it with a corpse.

Saying No wasn't easy at first. I'm a woman, after all, and a recovering people pleaser. But the more I said it, the better I felt. There's a feeling of great relief that comes with saying No to things that aren't serving my Priorities and Goals, even when it comes with a risk of disappointing others.

These days I say No way more than I say yes. In fact, I believe flexing my No muscle often has been key to my having the time and energy to grow in the parts of my life that I've declared important and to have a lot more fun and less stress while doing it. Get a load of all the things I said No to in the last month (and we were even out of the country for two of those weeks on vacation, where I was largely unplugged):

· Hosting a table at a fundraiser
· A consulting gig for a company looking to break into direct sales
· Three speaking gigs (including one keynote)
· Two dinner invitations

- An extra volunteer shift for our kids' musical production
- Three invitations for networking calls
- Two requests for personal coaching from team members who weren't investing time into their businesses
- An incentive trip I earned

And those are just the things I can remember. So *why* did I say No? Because they didn't serve one of my Priorities or Goals. Would I love to be able to help support every charity that reaches out to me for help? Absolutely, but there was no way that I could commit to filling a table when every spare moment needs to go into writing this book I am committed to. Is networking important for entrepreneurs, especially those in direct sales? It sure is, but only when the person who wants to network with you is in a position to help you expand your network and you think you can help them expand theirs. Do I love speaking gigs where I get to connect with an audience and leave them with nuggets that will help them enhance or even change their lives? Yes, I do, but not when it doesn't jibe with my brand and who I am as a person. Is a free trip to Cabo ever a bad idea? It is when it's going to cause me to short-change my parenting and spread myself too thin in a season with a lot of travel commitments already.

Check out this crazy cosmic phenomenon: when you say No to the things you don't want to do or can't do and instead serve your Priorities and Goals, you'll start getting more of what you do want. In the last year I've been getting a large number of invitations to participate in webinar series, in which all the participants commit to sharing the series with their networks. There must be loads of business development coaches who are telling entrepreneurs that this is a good way to grow their followers because I've been getting several requests a week over the last year.

When I started saying No, I started getting more of the types of opportunities I did want—like podcast interviews and requests to speak at events where the people I'm most interested in serving will be—and fewer of the types of webinars I didn't.

So *how* do you say No? I get that the thought of disappointing someone makes you uncomfortable or downright sick to your stomach. But once you learn how to do it, it's not so bad. And here's some great news: the more you say it, the easier it gets.

I've found the best way to decline an invitation or a request for my time is to be honest, authentic, and respectful, without hurting the other person's feelings. Truthfully share why you need to decline, without being defensive or apologetic or an asshole. And I include "sorry" only when I really mean it, instead of allowing it to be a knee-jerk response. I'm not sorry when I am protecting my time for my Priorities, so to say "sorry" would be disingenuous. Remember, the point is to be authentic.

Here are examples of the real words I used to say No in the following real-life invitations and requests for my time. There isn't a single, solitary word of BS in any of it.

Those webinars I've declined? *"I really respect what you're doing and hope it brings you a lot of success, but it's not the right opportunity for me and my business goals right now."*

The charity fundraiser? *"I love your mission and I'm honored you asked me to be involved. My plate is completely full, and if I take this on I won't be able to give it the time and attention it deserves. Wishing you a wildly successful event!"*

The lead volunteer at a youth theater production company? *"You know our whole family is so grateful for what you do, not just for our kids but the whole community. But there is no way I could fulfill the obligations of this position given everything else I'm committed to at this time. You thought of me because I don't half-ass anything, so I'm certainly not going to accept this honor and half-ass it. You deserve better."*

The team members who want my coaching? *"I'm thrilled that you have renewed goals for your business. I've loved providing resources and coaching in the past for you. But until you start consistently working your business and starting to grow your team, there's nothing more I can offer you at this time. I reserve my one-on-one coaching for those who are committed to consistently work their biz, and I'm so excited for us to get to work together in the future!"*

Cabo? *"This trip sounds amazing, and I'm so grateful that you invest so much in all of us to provide these kinds of experiences for a job well done. John and I have to decline, however, because this spring is already filled with loads of travel and business-building commitments, and we remain devoted to protecting time with our kids. I can't wait to hear about the unforgettable time our team members have!"*

The dinner? *"I've been running at warp speed lately to meet deadlines on a project I'm passionate about and to be there for our kids, who are very needy lately. Friday night is going to be my one night this week to unplug and breathe and get to bed at 8 p.m. We love being with you and would love to get together when I'm more rested and can enjoy your company. Let's look at dates in March."*

If we make our responses authentically personal, the other person probably won't take it personally. And if they do, they're reading more into your declination than you've truthfully relayed, and that's not your issue.

And please, promise me that even if you're having a hard time saying No, you'll find the balls to respond to the invitation or request. In my profession, where we talk to people about our products and the ability to grow their own turn-key business, we learn very quickly that social norms and common courtesy will get thrown out in order to avoid the perceived pain of having to say No. Standing someone up for meetings or calls, not responding to emails, or going into the Witness Protection Program. You're better than that.

I've learned this undeniable truth that I hope you take to heart: I will never be criticized by someone doing more than me; I will be criticized only by someone doing less. Think about that for a minute. Think of all the people who have criticized or judged you for saying No in some form or fashion. Are they people who are doing more than you? Hell to the No. Not ever. Because the people who are committed to living their truth in concert with their Priorities and Goals and are living productive and purpose-filled lives don't have the time to judge you.

YOUR STOP DOING LIST

Bestselling author and business/personal development expert Jim Collins preaches, "Stop doing lists are more important than to-do lists." And now that I've made you go through everything you're doing and helped you identify all the things to drop, delegate, and disown, it's time for you to make your Stop Doing List.

I've helped you hone your time-analyzing skills, so go back through everything you marked P or G and make extra sure they really do serve your Priorities and Goals. If they don't, you have to recategorize them.

The stuff you marked H or S? Revisit each entry and analyze it with the no-BS filter I've showed you and determine what you're going to delegate or delete altogether. And don't think you have to fix everything all at once. Start with the things that will give you the most instant relief. Is there a list of requests for your time you've been avoiding? Measure each one against your Priorities and Goals and then respond, putting your No muscle to work. Will hiring a housecleaner give you a nice big chunk of time back on your plate, along with more peace of mind? Go find one! And then every couple of weeks, find another delegating fix.

If you get pushback from your spouse or life partner on the decisions that you have to make together, take the time to share your Priorities and Goals with him or her, along with your hourly worth. It's powerful to show how investing in your own productivity and well-being makes financial sense. When I've had mentees with stubborn husbands who were reluctant to OK things like housecleaners or meal delivery services, I've coached them to give their hubbies four days to come up with a better solution. If they don't, then they made it clear they'll be moving forward with their plan. And they did.

Remember Sarah and Emily and the huge strides they made when they started Focusing their time on their Priorities and Goals? A big part of their breakthroughs was their Stop Doing List. They both learned to flex their No muscles instead of spending their time on the Shoulds and the things they Hate.

Emily stopped volunteering in five classrooms and stopped

going on field trips for all five kids. I joked with Emily that if I was doing that, I'd drink too.

"It's ridiculous the pressure I put on myself," she remembers. "I was doing it because I thought I was supposed to, but there were tons of resources for the kids at the school, and they didn't even want me on their field trips." Now Emily spends that time doing things one-on-one with her kids, really connecting with them instead of filling a role of school volunteer that she pressured herself into playing.

In her business she stopped doing everything for her team members and Focused on the parts of her business that only she could. This made her team feel more empowered and more successful and made Emily more productive and less resentful. She also stopped doing everything that she could hire an assistant to do. This allowed her to spend her work time on things that would continue to grow her business and keep giving her more time to serve her Priority of putting her health and well-being first. She even joined an orchestra and a choir.

"It's amazing the other things you can have time for—more fulfilling things—when you stop doing all the things that you shouldn't be doing."

When Emily faced another bout of cancer in 2018, it was without alcohol and with more clarity about how to get through the fight. "Because I knew how to Focus on my Priorities, I knew that in order to get through this, I had to ask for help. I used to think that was a sign of weakness. Now I know it's a smart way to live."

She hired more help with the kids, letting go of the BS that she Should be the one always chauffeuring them around, allowed her friends to set up a meal train, and got really honest with her husband about what she needed him to do.

We've already talked about how Sarah relinquished her control-freak tendencies and started delegating what was on her plate to an assistant, a housecleaner, collaboration partners at work, and her husband. She also learned to say No to all the things that she had been doing, not because she really wanted to, but because she thought she Should to play the role her family, friends, and community had come to expect.

Sarah started saying No to all the requests to chair this committee and that auction, and said Yes only to activities that would allow her to spend more time with her kids, like coaching their short-season sports team. She also learned how to say No to the huge Irish and Italian families that she and Kenny come from. This not only gave her back loads of time but also allowed her to enjoy holidays again. "I used to think I had to go to four houses before we could actually go out to trick-or-treat, every school program for every kid in the family, and three places for Mother's Day—the day that's supposed to be for me," she says now with a laugh. "I was doing what I thought I Should be doing as a good daughter and niece and sister. I was trying to be there for everyone else, but I wasn't living the life I wanted to live."

Since I came up with this time analysis process, I've been taking myself through it at least every six months. And when I start to feel stressed and that my schedule is out of control, I know it's time to do it again. I encourage you to do the same.

IT'S ABOUT MORE THAN TIME

I've had you do an analysis of what to edit out of your life primarily because of a mathematical equation and what your time is worth. Yet there's one more valuation I want you to think about: What's your mental well-being worth? Putting our time into all these Hates and Shoulds not only keeps us from getting to what we really want to do, it can also leave us feeling like we don't have control over our lives and, for many of us, cause or exacerbate depression.

Depression affects one in eight women, and women are twice as likely to suffer from it than men. I can't help but think it's in part because we put so damn much pressure on ourselves to do it all and be it all. And when we unavoidably come up short or aren't living in concert with our true Priorities and Goals—our true desires—it can put us in a funk or a full-blown depression.

It's happened to me, more than once. When I look back throughout my adult life—with the exception of my stints with postpartum depression that were about sleep deprivation and chemicals gone haywire—every time I've felt depressed, it's because there were too many things in my life that I either Hated or was doing solely because I thought it was something I Should be doing. Remember that suite at the Four Seasons in Vegas? Yep, I was depressed when I got there, and figuring out the process of what I really wanted and where I was going to Focus my time was the beginning of getting me out of it.

And it's not just mere mortals like us; even the most successful women, with an unlimited amount of resources available at their fingertips, can find themselves depressed when they're not living their truth. In a talk in 2015 at the Emotion Revolution Summit at Yale University, Lady Gaga shared her history of anxiety and depression and how learning her limits and saying No to all the things she didn't want to do was a big help. She said that she found herself unhappy amid her immense success because she was "selling fragrances, spending days shaking people's hands, and smiling and taking selfies. It feels shallow to my existence.

"I feel sad when I'm overworked and I've just become a money-making machine, and that my passion and my creativity take a back seat," she said, obviously referencing some of her Priorities. How did she fix it? She started to say No. How's this for a brilliant Gaga truthbomb: "It's your right to curate your own life."

Here's one from me: I don't care how gorgeous and expensive your china is; if there's too much on your plate, you're gonna collapse like a flimsy paper one at a Thanksgiving buffet.

Choose wisely. Say No. Stop doing so damn much and Focus on what really matters to you. As Lady Gaga said at Yale, "Our self-worth is not defined by the things we say Yes to, but by the things we say No to."

Five

PROTECT YOURSELF

*You cannot continue to move forward in your life
to the level you need to be if you're surrounded
by energy that brings you down, that sucks
the life force from you.*

—Oprah Winfrey

We've just spent a lot of time together figuring out where your time goes and where it's no longer going to go. And it's going to change your life. But Having It All requires more than protecting your time. It's also about learning where to Focus our emotions and thoughts. If we want to have the energy and the strength to build the lives we really want, we must learn to protect ourselves from negative emotions and thoughts and remove ourselves from—or at least recategorize—destructive relationships.

I'm a big fan of bestselling author Elizabeth Gilbert, a fiction writer who has also become a personal development catalyst. Liz has a vibrant and vocal Facebook community, where she shares so many gems. One post in particular was huge for me. She said that she always thought of herself as having low energy. But then one day it dawned on her—she wasn't low energy. She had allowed her energy to be zapped by all the emotional bullshit that wasn't serving her. Hello, Epiphany! How many things do we let drain us, causing us to lose our footing, our dedication to becoming the best version of ourselves, our Focus?

The amount of time and energy and emotion I have wasted over the years is staggering. On thoughts that didn't serve me, relationships that left me feeling annihilated instead of empowered, and attempts to be all things to all people. I don't want you to waste any more of your precious time on Earth on any of this stuff, so I want to take you through the principles I've adopted to ditch emotional drains. It's not easy, and it can come with some heartbreak. But I'm here to assure you that it's all worth it. Because who you get to be without all this baggage is so much stronger and more effective in all parts of your life and so much happier.

DON'T TAKE IT PERSONALLY

Back in my early thirties, I found Don Miguel Ruiz's seminal book, *The Four Agreements*. It was life-changing for me. Not overnight, as we often wish in the pursuit of personal development, but instrumental in my quest to let go of self-limiting beliefs and evolve into a more empowered and fulfilled me. I reread it every winter, curled up in a self-indulgent day devoted to shedding the negative and welcoming in all that's good. I highly recommend you try it. Not just the book but the time to dig into it, fuzzy blanket and all.

The Second Agreement commands, "Don't Take Anything Personally." Ruiz writes:

Nothing others do is because of you. What others say and do is a projection of their own reality, their own dream. When you are immune to the opinions and actions of others, you won't be the victim of needless suffering.

Think about it: How often do you let people's actions or inactions dictate your mood or your self-worth? It's compounded by the fact that most of us are walking around judging ourselves so harshly. How we feel on the inside can't help but spill out and onto our relationships. So we're all walking around being Judgy McJudgerson, and allowing it to wound us when we're on the receiving end.

Taking things personally used to be my knee-jerk reaction. I'm sure it has something to do with me being the baby of four kids and feeling ganged up on or left out a lot. Or, perhaps, me simply being a human. Whatever the reason, after reading Ruiz, I stopped beating myself up over the fact that I allowed it to get to me. Taking things personally was widespread enough to be one of the four friggin' agreements in the treatise on ancient Toltec wisdom, so who was I to think I could automatically dodge that bullet? This wisdom made it easier for me to recognize when I was doing it and to stop that shit. It not only improved my relationships, it also freed up a whole bunch of emotional space for happy instead of heavy. And the lighter and brighter we feel, the easier it is to go after what we want.

I have friends who are always late. We all do. I used to tell myself the story that it was because they didn't value my time. But when I took myself out of the equation and instead accepted that it was simply part of who they were, it was no longer frustrating or hurtful. It was an adorable quirk that I embraced and planned for.

A family member used to compare me to another family member often, pointing out how much better she was at juggling the various aspects of motherhood. When I stopped receiving these comments as personal jabs, I was able to do what my natural inclination had always been—to celebrate, cheer on, and be inspired by what this incredible ball-juggling, craft-making, cooking, baking, gift-giving, professional-level photography-ing, super-mommy-ing marvel did on a daily basis.

This whole not-taking-it-personally thing gets easier over time. The kinder I become with myself, the more comfortable and confident I am in my skin, the more I spend my time doing things that light me up, the less likely I am to experience things as a victim. Here's a recent example. Earlier this year I had surgery. Nothing serious, but a significant procedure that had me under for several hours nonetheless. Oh, hell, I'm an open book, and we've known each other a while now, so I might as well tell you: I had a breast reduction. And some of the people I'm closest to who knew about it didn't check in on me.

A few years ago, I guarantee it would've sent me into a spiral of "Don't they care?" or something even darker. But now that I've stopped holding myself up to an unattainable level of keeping on top of everything and everyone—and recognizing that nobody else can either—I didn't take it personally. Because it wasn't about how they felt about me. It was that their plates were filled with a whole bunch of stuff, and they were doing their best. Just like the rest of us.

If we're taking something personally, we should ask ourselves if it makes sense to talk it out. I get it—that can be scary, because the answer might not be what we want to hear. But we're taking it personally anyway, so what's the worst that can happen? After experiencing enormous success in my business, I was feeling lonely, despite tens of thousands of people on my team and more than triple that working with the company. I was feeling left out of a lot of collaboration in my work unless I was the one to spearhead it. It made me feel like the second grader who wasn't getting picked for kickball at recess. Instead of acting like a mopey little girl, I decided to put on my big-girl panties and asked some of my colleagues why they didn't include me in any of their efforts. Not in an accusatory way, but out of curiosity, sharing how much collaboration feeds my soul.

To my surprise, the reasons weren't about me but about how they felt about themselves. "You're so successful; I figured you wouldn't want to do something with us," I remember one of my team members saying. "You're always coming up with such great stuff," another said. "I just never thought you'd want to spend the time doing things like this with us."

They were thrilled to know that I considered them equal colleagues with whom I wanted to join forces. See, it wasn't personal, but I could've walked around thinking that forever. And because I found the guts to ask, it led to super fun and fulfilling group efforts I would have otherwise missed out on.

Since our natural inclination as humans is to take things personally, I think we all need to do a better job of being clear when the things we're doing—or aren't doing—aren't personal. While I was growing my business, I had to explain to several friends and family members that the reason I wasn't able to call or text or hang out as much was because I was juggling kids and work and getting in some exercise and practicing basic hygiene. But with some people I didn't have that conversation early enough, waiting until after I had to decline several invitations or an unusually long time had passed before I returned their calls. If I'm honest with myself, it's because I feared it would make me appear weak. Back then I was still holding on to the illusion that somewhere along the line I should've found that Wonder Woman costume and stuffed my postpartum ass into it. I wish I could go back and be crystal clear right out of the gate about why I was so committed to what I was working toward and that it would mean I wouldn't be as available as much as they were used to.

Some of them still took it personally because what I was really saying was "You're not a Priority for me right now." But the emphasis was on the "right now," and my relationships that have gone the distance are ones in which we show each other grace and understanding that sometimes a girl's gotta put her whole heart and soul into something. And when she emerges, she'll be an even more interesting, confident, wiser version of herself who adds that much more to the relationship.

ASSUME POSITIVE INTENT

We've all heard the wordplay catchphrase "Assume and you make an ass out of you and me," and I think it's a key concept to protecting our thoughts and emotions. The ancient Toltecs agree, so much so that "Don't Make Assumptions" is the Third Agreement in Ruiz's book.

How much needless drama is created because of the bullshit stories we make up in our heads? We don't hear from a friend and then make up a story of why she's mad at us, when in reality she simply was too busy to dig herself out from under a bunch of kid stuff, a pile of laundry, and a root canal. Someone doesn't respond to a text or email or voicemail as quickly as we think they should. Or declines an invite to sit at our table at a charity event. Or doesn't invite us to a girls' trip. Or ever invite us to a post-work dinner. And I could go on and on.

It's pretty hard for humans to stop making assumptions. But imagine how much it would improve our lives if we all abided by this simple yet undeniable drama-reducing credo: Assume positive intent.

The risk of assuming the worst is rampant in a business like mine, and it's helped me hone my Third Agreement skills. Since direct sales requires us to constantly reach out to people we know or are referred to, nonresponses often get interpreted as a personal condemnation, which can dampen our confidence, slow down our efforts, and keep us from reaching out to that person— or anyone else—ever again. Yet there are countless examples of the silence being caused by personal issues or crises or just a bad day. I've had people thank me for reaching out again (and sometimes again and again), grateful that I caught them at just the right time to discuss our products or how to start their own business. If I had assumed the worst, I would've missed out on these customers and team members.

And if it seems impossible to assume positive intent without knowing for sure, I encourage us to ask questions. A dear friend interpreted a text message of mine to mean something accusatory and unkind. She posted an adorable picture that included me on Facebook along with a message that talked about how grateful she was for the friendships and collaboration in our business. My text thanked her for posting the pic and told her that I hoped she got "a lot of traction from it." It turns out she interpreted my text as an implication that she was using me to get social media play. That wasn't my intent at all; the purpose of my text was to relay a bravo-and-go-get-'em-girl kind of message because it was a really well-done post. It was definitely not received that way, and instead of asking for clarification, she assumed the worst.

Weeks later, when I asked her to lunch and asked her why she had been so cold to me, the emotional tornado had already done a number on her feelings, as she viewed me and many things I had done over those weeks through a negative lens. I was shocked and devastated that, after years of close friendship, she didn't give me the benefit of the doubt or at least have a conversation about it. Now, shame on me for not confronting the coldness right when it started to avoid an avalanche of resentment on her part. But I also wish she would've talked to me about it. So much heartache on both sides could have been avoided if, as Ruiz wrote, we had found the courage to ask questions and "communicate with others as clearly as you can to avoid misunderstandings, sadness and drama. With just this one agreement, you can completely transform your life." Those are words to live by.

I learned to triple-read my texts to try to determine if something could be interpreted in any other way than I intended, and I vowed not to sit on icky feelings with those I love without having a conversation. I also extended grace and forgiveness to her because I've been in her shoes and jumped to a negative conclusion. Thankfully, we're both self-reflective people who love each other and treasure our friendship. I'm so grateful that our overdue pow-wow led us to tearfully vow that open communication is a non-negotiable in our relationship.

YOU CAN'T BE EVERYONE'S CUP OF TEA

Hello, my name is Romi, and I'm a recovering people pleaser. As the youngest of four, I spent so much time and effort throughout the first three decades of my life trying to get my siblings to like and accept me. I got in the habit of pushing down my personality and desires to try to be someone they would love and unconditionally accept. I also grew up in a family environment that often measured one kid against the other, and I learned early on that I didn't want to be the one negatively talked about. So I tried to turn myself into this person who was always beyond reproach—in other words, someone who was perfect—which is an unattainable enterprise whether you're twelve or twenty-two or forty-two or eighty-two. And in case you're wondering, I failed miserably.

This people pleasing bled into my friendships, professional endeavors, even how I've tried to change myself to fit in with other moms. I've held my tongue, stuffed my round peg into some really uncomfortable square holes, and made myself smaller so people would like or love me.

How draining it is to go through life trying to please everyone and trying to make sure everyone likes you. And what a waste. Cause that ain't ever gonna happen.

Thankfully, one day it dawned on me that trying to contort myself wasn't leading to deep, meaningful, or rewarding relationships. Instead it was exhausting and heartbreaking and making me feel like a fraud. Around my fortieth birthday, I came to the realization that I was never going to be everyone's cup of tea, and I was OK with that because that's not why I was here. What a relief! To be able to remove "Make sure everyone likes me and loves me" from my to-do list freed up so much emotional energy and allowed me to fully celebrate all that I had become and achieved and all I had to offer the right people.

I will never have any control over other people's opinions of me. All I can control is my opinion of me as I do the work it takes to keep falling more in love with who I am. I don't hold any animosity toward anyone who doesn't dig what I put out in the world. I simply accept that we aren't a match. And that's OK.

There's not only great freedom that comes with this realization but also with its corollary: not everyone will be *my* cup of tea. And that's OK too.

I keep a mantra close to me that I love because it makes me giggle and reminds me to stop caring what other people think:

You will be too much for some people. Those aren't your people.

And here's the most amazing thing—when we stop trying to be everyone's cup of tea, we find more of our people and are able to give them our whole uncensored selves. That's what they deserve, and so do we.

LET GO OF DRAINING RELATIONSHIPS

There's another mantra I love and refer to often: *Stick with the people who pull the magic out of you and not the madness.*

If we fill our lives with people who drain or diminish us, how will we ever have room for the people who will elevate us and those we're supposed to lift up? How can we possibly have the mindshare for everything that's on our to-do lists to slay our goals? We can't. Which is why sometimes we have to let go of our relationships with unrelenting critics, energy suckers, negative Nellies, uninvited competitors, and those we simply can't please.

One of the most heartbreaking parts of my life and my husband's has been accepting that some people aren't supposed to be in our lives forever. But we learned to Focus on celebrating the good memories and feeling gratitude for the good times, everything they did for us and taught us, and, we hope, vice versa.

All relationships (friends, family, romantic, and professional) aren't always easy; they go through seasons. And we humans make mistakes and can and should attempt to do what's necessary to make things right. But sometimes there's no repairing what was. And sometimes we've got to recognize that a relationship that once was healthy and elevating—or that we had hoped one day would be—simply doesn't work, and it's time to break up.

It takes courage to say goodbye to relationships, and to understand that when we do, we're not just letting go of the other person but also saying goodbye to the person we allow ourselves to become when we spend time with him or her. Even if that version of you isn't your best, it's familiar, and it's hard to let go of what we're used to.

I'm not going to sugarcoat it: breaking up with people can be brutal, and it has been for this youngest child, recovering people pleaser. But I've found it to be so much easier if you take a deep, critical look at your relationship and who you are in it, and then decide how you want to say goodbye. As I've mentioned, before I reached my forties, I tolerated a lot more than I should have in an attempt to take what I thought was the easy route and avoid conflict at any cost. But that all changed after hitting my fifth decade. Holy shit, that sounds old, but the forties truly can be a magical time for women to finally declare that this is who I am and who I'm not, and this is what I want and these are my boundaries, dammit. (And just so you know, if you're younger than forty, I know you can get there earlier than I did if you work at it.)

Some of my long-term relationships that I had invested so much blood, sweat, and tears in had reached such a painful point that there was no denying it wasn't healthy for them or me. It was hard—gut-wrenching, really—to let go of the "what if" fantasy game. Maybe you've played it too. What if I could just learn to ignore her negativity and snide comments? What if he could learn to love and accept me for who I am? What if she didn't have to make me feel small to make herself feel big? But thanks to therapy, lots of reading, and honestly answering a list of questions I compiled, I was able to come to terms with relationships that were giving me pain. I still pull them out every time I find myself in a relationship that I can't seem to make better, whether in business or other parts of my life. I hope it helps you get clarity too.

Grab a journal and write down the answers to these questions, without judgment and without overanalyzing or making excuses for you or the other person. You can also download a printable version of these relationship questions at romineustadt.com/resources. I've found that what comes out of us and onto the paper first is the most honest reflection of what we're really feeling.

Can I be completely myself around this person?

Does this person make me feel elevated or drained?

Do I feel more confident around this person, or do I feel crushed?

Do I routinely feel like I can't do anything right in this person's eyes?

Do I make myself smaller to make him or her feel bigger?

Are there rules to this relationship that I can't or am unwilling to follow?

Did our relationship change, and if so, when?

Is this relationship rooted in something that's no longer relevant to me or both of us?

Do I feel I can openly communicate with this person about my thoughts, feelings, and desires, and is that open communication reciprocated? If not, why?

Does this relationship bring out the best of me? Does it bring out the worst?

What role do I play in this dysfunction?

Does the thought of not having this person in my life give me a feeling of relief?

I've often found that by the time I'm asking myself these questions, deep down I already know the answers, and the exercise is there to give me permission to let go. How you do it depends on the dynamics of that particular relationship and the answers to the previous questions.

This exercise can also help us uncover patterns in our relationships and dig deep to find out why. For example, I discovered I have a history of relationships that "worked" as long as I lived up to the other person's idea of what I should be and what I should do. But when I was being authentic in the relationship—instead of trying to play the perfect people-pleaser role I learned as a child—it caused conflict and disappointment in the other person.

Because that dynamic was familiar to me as a child, while it was painful, it was what I knew. And the more critical someone was of me, the more I tried to turn myself into a pretzel to meet their expectations. Even when it's unhealthy or destructive, what's familiar is comfortable.

It also helped me see when a relationship changed because one or both of us had changed—professions, marital or parenting status, level of success, lifestyle, or hobbies. Sometimes two people no longer have as much in common. And sometimes life changes the power (or perceived power) balance in a relationship or can cause resentment. It's not anyone's fault; it just is. If the relationship is no longer working because one or both of you are being who you are and that no longer works, it's not a failure. It's an evolution. Not all relationships are meant for forever.

The bravest—and yes, the hardest—way to get out of a relationship that isn't working is to have a conversation about how it's making you feel. Using your answers from the previous questions, make "I feel" statements; as in "I feel like I can't do anything right in this relationship," or "I feel that you belittle my dreams instead of supporting me." Best-case scenario is that bringing your feelings to light will lead the other person to change her behavior and illuminate ways that you need to change your behavior, with both of you moving on to an even deeper understanding of each other.

Or maybe the relationship has to change and be limited to the kinds of interactions that are comfortable for you both. Worst case is that you come to the undeniable conclusion that the other person simply doesn't view the world or you in the ways that makes it possible for you to have a relationship. Having the courage to acknowledge, "I can't put my time or emotional energy into someone who doesn't value me/doesn't support me/[fill in the blank]," will allow each of you to let go and Focus on positive relationships that elevate you both.

Sometimes the other person won't accept your attempts to talk things through and avoids frank and constructive communication at all costs. Or an honest, constructive conversation isn't possible because the other person views any deeply personal conversation as confrontational. I've learned to accept that the kind of resolution I may be looking for simply won't happen. There's not much we can do with people who refuse to talk through feelings and end up stewing, giving us the cold shoulder, and even airing grievances behind our backs or—gasp—on social media. Sometimes the best way to let go is to stop trying. Remove yourself from interactions, or if you're forced to have them because of work or another group dynamic, engage only when absolutely necessary. Since the other person simply won't view conflict resolution as anything more than confrontation, you've got to change the way you think of that person and remove any vulnerability from your relationship. And because he or she is an avoider, why your dynamic has changed will likely never come up.

A friend of mine decided to limit her amount of exposure to a co-worker after years of phone calls and voicemails that were "rude and scathing, filled with name-calling and a refusal to listen to my point of view." My friend readily admitted that she didn't know everything and enjoyed conversations with co-workers that resulted in her viewing issues from a different perspective, learning new things, and compromising. But after years of trying to have calm and productive conversations with her colleague, my friend won't answer her calls and deletes her voice-mails. "I won't let this person steal the joy from the work I love and cause me to doubt myself, my abilities, and my worth."

If you can't have the frank conversation because the other person can't or won't, it's often helpful to get all your feelings out so you can move on. Write it all down in a respectful "I feel" approach that says everything that you want to say. And then don't send it! It's healthy to commit emotions like anger, hurt, and resentment to the written page as long as you don't give it to the object of those feelings. Get it all out and then channel your inner Elsa from *Frozen* and let it go. Here's a pro tip: write away and then burn it or shred it for that extra release.

What if *you're* the avoider? You've got to ask yourself why you're dodging a conversation. Are you afraid you'll learn that you're at fault too? Tough, I know, but how can we expect others to own their behavior and learn from it if we're not willing to do the same? I'm not suggesting any of us subject ourselves to confrontations that we know from prior experience can end up abusive or an attempt in futility. But if a conversation can help you work through your relationship and let it go more elegantly while learning valuable lessons, you've got to find your balls and do it.

If you can't move past the issues in the relationship, let that person go with love. It's important to take time to grieve the loss, because it is a death. And no matter how mad or hurt you are, you've got to let go of all the negative, the wronged feelings, the resentment. As Buddha put it, "Holding on to anger is like grasping a hot coal with the intent of throwing it at someone else—you are the one who gets burned."

WHEN THE FAMILY BOND
IS BROKEN

All of this emotionally gut-wrenching stuff is exponentially harder when the broken relationships are with family members. It's devastating when you feel that family doesn't know your heart. Many of you may believe that no matter what, family relationships are sacred, and you don't "break up" with family, no matter what. I used to think that way, but then I learned how my uncle and cousin had been the source of a lot of pain in my father's life and, even after his death, how they tried to avoid paying my mom for his part of the family furniture business. I vowed that in order for me to invest my heart and time in family members, I had to apply the same standards and stay true to the same boundaries I use for everyone else.

For some of my relatives, I've had to recategorize our relationships, telling myself a new story about the role we play in each other's lives. I've asked myself the questions I shared with you, and it's clear we don't work. And with another, I had to cut off my relationship because I no longer felt emotionally safe, and her presence was negatively affecting our kids. After decades of being hurt and being told all the ways I had disappointed her, I could no longer bear how this relationship made me feel broken and unlovable. I didn't like who I was around her, always feeling like I couldn't be myself and that I was constantly being measured by my mistakes. I knew it was the right decision to let go when I didn't feel blame or anger. I had simply reached my limit of what my heart could take and got crystal clear on what I wanted to model for Nate and Bebe. A loss like this is a death, and to be honest, I'm still—years later—going through the grieving process. When sadness rises up, I think of happy memories we shared, and then I send love and good wishes her way. Because I do wish her the very best, even though we didn't bring out the best in one another.

We're the only gatekeepers we'll ever have to protect our emotions, so we have to take this job seriously and show up, especially when it's hard. When I finally accepted this fact and showed up diligently and courageously every day, that's when I found the energy and emotions to Focus on what mattered, and it elevated my life. Would I still be this successful if I had avoided this hard work? Maybe. But I wouldn't be filled with peace and fulfillment, and I sure wouldn't enjoy it as much. And I'm convinced I wouldn't have been able to become a more authentic me who's able to attract more opportunities and deeper and more meaningful relationships with the people who bring out the best in me and I them.

I've found my people, the ones who pull the magic out of me. And because I've let go of the ones who don't, I've got a lot more magic to give. And I like to think that those I've said goodbye to do too.

DEVELOP HABITS
THAT SERVE YOU

*What we do every day matters more than
what we do once in a while.*

—Gretchen Rubin

W hat if I told you that there were things you could do that would make you more productive, improve your health, reduce your stress, and make you feel like you had more of your shit together? Sign you up, right? But I have to be honest: you'll have to do things that, at first, might feel a little uncomfortable because they're different from what you've been doing. And they might feel like you're adding something else to your already full plate. But I beg you to keep an open mind.

Habits have gotten a bad rap because, let's face it, we've all found them pretty damn hard to stick to. And when we have a track record of stumbles, it's hard to think of tackling another one with enthusiasm and confidence. So first I want to get in your head and help you get in the habit of rethinking habits (see what I did there?). I had to change my mindset, and so can you.

Habits help us solve problems. And if you're committed to incorporating them into your life, they'll help you Have It All.

Let me be clear: I'm not a habits expert. What I have become good at is figuring out what tweaks and changes I need to do—both big and little—to make it easier for me to accomplish everything I want to and live the way I want to live.

Experts in the field have said that the key to habits is having them become our automatic default behavior. I have a really hard time thinking of them this way, as do a lot of the women I've coached and mentored. To me, habits are the decisions we consciously make every day, all day long. And it's freaking hard.

Let me also be clear: I fall down and backslide as much as the next girl. But that's OK, because habits are about doing the right thing *most* of the time. When you go a little or a lot off course, it isn't fatal. The key is to be committed to keeping our habit streak going, so if we screw up/fall off the horse/blow chunks all over our best intentions, we can recover if we don't do it for a second day in a row. Because two days can easily turn into two months. And then before you know it, you have to marshal the same amount of motivation and discipline to restart the habit. We don't need to do that to ourselves, do we?

Too often we put so much pressure on ourselves to make these huge changes—even overnight—and then beat ourselves up when we're not able to do it. We can't underestimate the importance of making small, incremental changes to our daily habits. Did we expect our kids to go from rolling around on the floor to speed-walking across a room like zombie monsters overnight? Nope.

They had to learn to sit up and then crawl and then fall flat on their faces, then stand holding on, stand unassisted, walk while holding our hands, then walk alone. Teetering and tripping many times along the way.

So why the hell do we expect ourselves to wake up one day and declare we're going to make sweeping changes, like quitting smoking, cutting out sugar, and going to the gym every day? To make matters worse, we're ruthless with ourselves when we're not able to successfully triumph in the face of unrealistic expectations.

Small changes add up, maybe not right in the moment to feed our desires for instant gratification, but over time. And the daily decisions we make add up and either sabotage us or allow us to serve our Priorities and reach our Goals. The best part is that the choice is ours.

Here's a truth bomb for you: this book or a magazine article or your doctor or a podcast or even Oprah can't make you modify or start a habit . . . unless you want it badly enough. You must have a big enough desire for what the habit will bring you, or you won't do it. Well, maybe sheer willpower will get you to do it for a few days or even a few weeks. But for the long haul, I know from experience, and so do you, that it ain't gonna happen.

HOW PAINFUL IS YOUR PAIN?

I think a lot of us walk around thinking we lack discipline, and it's either a genetic flaw or a weakness in our character. I disagree. I believe we can cultivate discipline. We need look no further than Freud's pleasure principle to understand this. We humans seek to avoid pain and seek pleasure. I've been able to identify the habits I need to adopt by figuring out what's causing me pain so I could eliminate it and experience pleasure. It's as simple as that. And the pain has to be significant enough to get me to be disciplined enough to consistently take action, especially when the action is hard or uncomfortable or goes against what everyone else seems to be doing.

Here's some proof, three generations of it. A grandmother, a mother, and a daughter were able to change their habits when the pain was big enough and they wanted to eliminate it badly enough.

My mom, Dee, started smoking at sixteen (she blames my dad for getting her hooked) and smoked for more than fifty years. While my dad quit one day after his third child was born because he was scared to death that he'd never see his son grow up, my mom kept puffing away through all her pregnancies, in the car with the windows up and her kids in the back, from morning until night. Secondhand what? She'd make attempts, but none of them stuck. It wasn't until she was in her seventies, in the hospital and in desperate need of a stent, when the doctor showed her an image of her heart. "If you don't stop smoking, your aorta is going to rupture," she said. "But if you stop, it can reverse back to normal size, even after all these years of smoking." Mom never smoked again. Now, at eighty-nine, she's still smoke-free but readily admits that "if I wasn't scared to death of croaking, I'd light up in a heartbeat." Yet she doesn't, because the pain is too big.

I've always been fascinated by nutrition and knew, even as a kid, that there was something fishy about counting iceberg lettuce as the vegetable at dinner and eating Pop-Tarts for breakfast. And I've always had a feeling that refined sugar was my kryptonite, long before researchers were claiming it was eight times more addictive than cocaine. I'd quit sugar for periods of time, primarily to drop weight to fit into a dress for a big event, but once the zipper went up and the event had passed, I'd fall back in the habit of indulging "just this once." Once would become once or twice a week, and then escalate to frequent hits to get my fix. The months between Halloween and New Year's were always the worst. It was only when the negative effects escalated, and it became undeniable that this kryptonite was zapping my energy, making me a royal bitch and unable to think clearly, that the pain got big enough for me to say enough. It was more important to me that I had the energy and stable brain to live my full life. I took refined sugar completely out of my diet and stopped giving that crap any power over me. And on the rare occasions that I have a little taste of dessert, it makes me feel so awful, I'm quickly reminded why I make this habit nonnegotiable.

Like the rest of her family, my daughter, Bebe, has a love affair with food and always has. In fact, when the nurse put her on my chest, she didn't even take the time to look at me and say hello like her big brother had. Instead—in what can only be described as a maniacal, urgent search for my nipple—she went straight for her first meal with such gusto I thought I was going to lose a breast. Bebe is most passionate about refined carbs of all kinds, especially bread. Gee, I wonder where she got that? But when she was around seven years old, she started having tummy and skin issues. Like any good naturopathic doctor daddy, John looked first at dietary causes. As much as he tried to encourage her to give up gluten for a couple of weeks to determine if it was the culprit (as it was for her mother and that former chain-smoker grandmother), our strong-willed girl wouldn't do it. Bebe didn't stop eating gluten until the stomachaches and acid reflux got so severe that they kept her from her beloved dancing, and the rash on her face got embarrassing enough. Within three days of no gluten, her stomach felt great and the rash was gone. Nearly four years later she's still gluten-free, indulging only occasionally with an amount she knows won't cause problems.

All three of us are capable of great discipline. Mom cleaned bathrooms in our house almost every single day of my childhood. Granted, there may be a bit of OCD at play, but that's some serious commitment. Bebe has spent hours upon hours practicing dance routines and musical theater numbers to the exclusion of other tempting distractions. And by the time you're reading this, I've written two books. So the reasons we didn't adopt and stay faithful to habits wasn't a lack of discipline. The pain had to get so big that it was bigger than the pain of adopting a new habit. Our desire for relief was bigger than our fear of discomfort.

FLIP THE STORY YOU'RE TELLING YOURSELF

Hopefully you're with me now and acknowledge that keeping to habits has less to do with discipline and more to do with how badly we want the outcome. And in order to change some existing habits and abandon others, we've also got to be willing to let go of some baggage. I'm talking about the thoughts you might have that might go something like "I've never been able to keep to a habit before. Why will this time be different?" Let's tell ourselves a different story, shall we?

Instead of talking to ourselves and others about our habits as drudgery filled to-dos, let's take ownership of our choices. Instead of "I *can't* eat sugar," say "I *don't* eat sugar." This habit isn't being imposed upon you; it's your choice. And something empowering happens when we talk about the benefits of our choices. "I *have* to wake up early" becomes "I *get* to wake up early to get a jump start on my day." "I *have* to work out" becomes "I *get* to make my health a priority and boost my energy."

And if "habit" is a dirty word for you, feel free to use another word. How about "ritual"? Check out the difference:

I'm focused on my habit of tackling my inbox in my first thirty minutes after lunch.

Or

I'm obsessed with my post-lunch ritual of grabbing tea and tackling my inbox for thirty minutes.

The first one... meh. The second one sounds almost indulgent, sexy, Insta-worthy.

HABITS THAT HAVE HELPED ME HAVE IT ALL

There's no doubt in my mind that I've been able to continue to grow as a success story and as a human because I've been willing to commit to habits in my life. They've been essential to solving problems. Please understand that I'm not suggesting you should adopt the following habits. But I want to walk you through some of the ones I've adopted to eliminate *my* pain points. Just like my All may look very different from yours, my habits may not be what you need to problem solve in your life. Once we get through mine, I'm going to walk you through how to identify what needs tweaking in your day-to-day life.

A handful of the habits I'm sharing involve technology to be more productive in our work hours and to get more sleep. But I have much more to say about how our devices can hijack our attention and our lives in the next chapter.

TAKE CONTROL OVER YOUR SCHEDULE

My life works because I schedule it. I'm able to do all the things I want to do because I know when I'm going to do them. Many of us think we lack motivation—me included—when the real problem is that we lack clarity over what we need to do and when. When I was growing my business and trying to raise humans and have time for John, myself, and a shower, I quickly learned that if I didn't have everything scheduled, there was no way I was going to get everything done that I needed to and have any time left over for me. If I had to make a decision in the moment of what to do next, I'd spend my valuable time trying to get organized, and I'd end up overwhelmed. What a waste of time and energy.

I've got to admit that I pushed back on this whole scheduling thing for a while after I left Corporate America. Remember, I had two professions where I was tied to the billable hour. Everything I did was measured by 0.6 or 0.25 hours. Once I was free of that,

I rebelled for a while from any formalized scheduling because I was so damn sick of it. That worked for about a week, and then it was clear I had to bring organization back. This is a mistake I think a lot of women make when they leave a traditional work situation or how they schedule their nonprofessional time. I had to come up with a process that worked for me and make it a habit. Nearly ten years later I still stick to it religiously.

I put everything that relates to my time and my kids' time in one place. I'm an iCal girl, but I know lots of women who are still tied to the old-school paper planners that work for them. Everything goes in there: anything to do with work (not just appointments but when I'm going to work on various tasks), personal appointments, workouts, kid events, time with my mom, dog stuff, social engagements, family time, date nights, everything. I categorize the entries according to professional, personal, and family.

It's one thing to put stuff on our calendars; it's a whole other thing to take the time to immerse ourselves in our schedules and partner with them. This may sound weird, but I think of my calendar as one of my assistants; without it, my life doesn't work. That's why every Sunday afternoon I have a date with my calendar to map out the coming week. I look at everything that's already on there from preplanning to recurring appointments, and I make sure that everything else that touches my life or my kids' lives is logged. I also use this time to calendar my kids' long-term commitments that have come through during the week. Anyone ever had a child or two in a musical theater production or competitive dance? Oy frickin' vey with the scheduling. I'm sure it's no worse than soccer or lacrosse or volleyball, so whatever extracurriculars your kids are in, I feel you (insert fist bump). I've found that putting it all in my calendar the week I get the info helps to keep me from getting overwhelmed and to better incorporate it into the rest of my life. Knowing where all the moving pieces are gives me peace. It's as simple as that. When I started this process, I turned it into a "me time" ritual. I gifted myself fifteen to thirty minutes to put on my current favorite music and grab a cup of tea and a snack. So even if I wasn't that excited about digging into my schedule, I looked forward to being left alone. Can the mamas out there relate? After a few months of seeing what a huge difference this time investment made to increase my productivity and reduce my anxiety—and what a disaster it was when I didn't take the time—I didn't need the ritual anymore to entice me to get it done.

This Sunday review is also another opportunity for me to measure what I've signed myself up for against my Priorities and Goals. I've learned that if I get an anxious feeling while reviewing my schedule, it means that I'm biting off too much. I go through everything and look for the things that are Shoulds and either delete or delegate them. For example, this week, knowing I had a lot of writing to do and a big product launch in my skincare business, I deleted a request from a colleague to pick my brain about my thoughts on a training series she wants to do. I also redlined a meeting at school to talk about mindfulness in parenting. Would I love to help everyone? Sure, but that's a half hour I could squeeze in a workout. Am I interested in improving my parenting skills? Lord knows I can use all the help I can get, but this week my parenting will be better served if I'm present for my kids when I'm with them, instead of stressed from trying to cram too much onto my plate. Giving advice to a colleague and going to a parenting meeting aren't going to serve my Priorities, so they gotta go.

No judgment, no regret. Just a delete, which is always quickly followed by relief.

Then John and I do our weekly "traffic meeting" to coordinate our schedules and juggle responsibilities. In usually less than fifteen minutes we're able to figure out who's going to take the kids to school on which days, who can be at the house for the plumber, where we need our blessed Linda to fill in the gaps. And where we have free time in common so we can go do something fun together. I'm lucky that John keeps a super-scheduled calendar too and also wants to avoid the pain of dropping balls. So he's never needed coaxing to spend this time together every week. But if he did, I would've created a ritual that we could enjoy together.

I quickly realized that focusing on my calendar once a week wasn't going to be enough, because a full life means life happens, and best-laid plans can turn to shit. A kid gets sick, the water heater goes out, a work crisis arises. So every day before I put my devices to bed, I spend five minutes looking at the next day's schedule. I juggle when necessary, check in with John or Linda if relevant, and get comfortable with what the next day holds.

It's important to add that John and I make sure to share appointments with each other. If he's taking Bebe to her dentist appointment, he still sends me a calendar invite that designates he's in charge. I categorize it as family instead of personal, but now I know not to schedule Bebe into anything at that time. We also know when we each have travel or local events that will tie us up, so we know one of us won't be available for anything else. We overshare our schedules because we've learned it's better to have too much info than too little, and it helps us avoid conflicts or missteps. Well, at least most of the time.

This super-scheduled way of living might have you asking,

"What about spontaneity, Sister?" Oh, spontaneity happens, but it just has to be scheduled. Go ahead, sing a chorus of Alanis Morissette's "Ironic," but it's enough freedom for me. Because I know where all the balls are and when I'm going to catch each one, I'm also able to schedule in free time where I can do whatever the hell I want—go for a walk, watch a show, get in extra reading, have coffee with a girlfriend, or enjoy some retail therapy.

And, yes, John and I have even scheduled romance. In addition to date nights, when we were in the thick of start-up mode in our businesses and our family, we even scheduled sex. Is that spontaneous? Nope. But it's how we made sure to find time for each other when we weren't co-parenting or hammering out logistics. There were nights we were still too tired to get busy, but at least we made it clear that we were still a Priority for each other. Time reserved to check in and fall asleep during pillow talk kept us close. Unless we're on vacation without the kids, our sex life doesn't often resemble a steamy scene in a movie. But our twenty-year love affair continues to get stronger all the time, so I'll take scheduled over steamy any day.

I don't see my well-defined schedule as rigid or limiting; just the opposite. It allows me to do more and enjoy what I'm doing more, which makes me feel more in control and free. Every minute I spend working my schedule helps me proactively live my life instead of reacting to it. Which helps me keep my Focus on my Priorities and Goals.

DO THE HARD STUFF FIRST

Humans will go to great lengths to avoid what's hard, which is why our to-do lists are often filled with the same labor-intensive and scary stuff week after week, while the easy tasks get crossed off daily for the win column. When left to our own devices, we humans will choose the option that requires the least effort. We want to be able to show forward motion, that we've accomplished something. But are we claiming victory over what matters? It's the hard stuff that's almost always what we need to be doing to serve our Priorities and Goals. Even if we have our schedules laid out like a carefully crafted mosaic, if we haven't committed to do the hard stuff first, it drastically reduces the likelihood we'll do what we've committed to.

When I'm blocking off chunks of time on Sundays, I designate what I'll be doing during that chunk, and the hard stuff always comes first. For some people, the hardest thing is getting themselves to exercise or doing house projects. For me, it's writing—whether it's books, blogs, trainings, or speeches. Don't get me wrong: I love to write, and there's nothing like getting in the flow. Yet I've learned that getting in the flow can be impossible after I've already devoted my fresh, energetic self to other tasks. Left to my own in-the-moment decision-making, I would choose just about everything else on my to-do list and even the things that aren't there to avoid the hardest work of creating something that might suck. That's why I've blocked off my mornings for me and my laptop and nothing else. It's the way I know I can set myself up for success.

When I have time scheduled for work, I'll do the tasks that are hardest for me first. Even ten years in, reaching out to people is still the hardest part for me, so that time has to be sacrosanct. And I don't get to move on to anything else until I've met my reach-out goal.

I've found that building in rewards for sticking to my schedule reinforces my commitment, like a rat in a science experiment. Get through my writing time? I get to have lunch while I look at a discount designer site or read a magazine. Get through my reach outs for my business? I get to grab a coffee and read or call a friend. Because I've set up a do-the-work-get-the-reward system, when I don't get the reward, I miss it. I also keep my goals visible—both on my goal/dream board and written in my journal—so I'm always thinking about how painful it will be if I don't accomplish what I really want. And let's be honest, the risk of having to repay my book advance doesn't hurt either.

When I realized my propensity for procrastination wasn't because I was weak but because I was human, I felt more empowered. Scheduling myself according to my humanity—and not in spite of it—has made an enormous difference in how much I'm able to accomplish.

START THE DAY THE RIGHT WAY

It's horrible to start the day feeling like we're already behind or throwing ourselves immediately into our to-do lists. I learned years ago that unless I woke up at least an hour before the kids, I'd start my day feeling like Indiana Jones running through the tunnel being chased by an enormous boulder. I also realized that waking up and immediately turning to my phone and my inbox was a recipe for an anxiety-filled, reactive day. The day I declared "Enough!" and took control over my mornings was life-changing. How we wake up sets the mood for our entire day. And here's the beautiful part: each of us gets to decide how our day starts, what our mood will be. I choose to start mine with gratitude, positivity, and inspiration.

First, this required me to stop using my phone as an alarm clock. I fully recognize that I don't possess the willpower to pick up my phone to turn off the alarm and not check any one of the numerous tempting apps. I use a real alarm clock, and I put my phone in another room. Even when I travel, I go old school and ask for a wake-up call or use the alarm clock in the hotel room. I set my phone alarm as a backup, but I put it in the bathroom. What a joy it is to wake up and avoid having to assert any will-power first thing in the morning.

And then my morning ritual starts, one I've been doing for years. It is a ritual, not just because that sounds better to me than "habit" but because it feels spiritual to me. Once I open my eyes, I first say "thank you" to God and the Universe for giving me another day, and then I think about one or two additional things I'm grateful for. This morning I expressed gratitude that we'd gotten so much rain so the view of the canyon from my bedroom window was filled with gorgeous shades of green. I was also grateful that the stuffy nose I'd gone to bed with was gone. Nothing monumental, but I'm immediately focusing on the positive. Then I take deep breaths and do a scan of my body—something I learned from yoga classes—which helps center me and, I believe, helps me be more present throughout the day. I set my intention for the day, which isn't a review of my to-do list but how I want to approach the gift of the next sixteen or so hours. Today my intention was Peace because I have so much to accomplish, including a big event I'm cohosting and a lot of variables. If I approach the day through a lens of Peace, everything will work out, and I'll be present and enjoy it and rise to whatever the day demands. I take a few seconds to stretch, and then I follow best-selling author Mel Robbins's famous 5-Second Rule to count down 5-4-3-2-1 to get out of bed.

I go down to our kitchen, say good morning to our labradoodle and John (he gets up even earlier than I do), and make celery juice if my dear hubby hasn't already done it (yep, we're on that bandwagon and swear by it). I read or listen to a book while I drink my juice, and once I'm done, I set my phone alarm for twenty minutes (the time I have to wait before I can have my coffee so the celery juice can do what it's supposed to). Until it's my treasured coffee time, I get those twenty minutes to check my phone notifications and read and respond to email. Once I have coffee in hand, I throw on my clothes and help the kids get ready for school. By the time those buggers are awake and needing me for anything, I've already had plenty of time to myself and a little with John, I've practiced valuable self-care, I've cleaned out my inbox, and I've started caffeinating myself.

Equally important to this ritual is doing everything possible to blow it to bits one day over the weekend. I love lazy mornings in bed, and once our kids were old enough to fend for themselves in the morning, I started luxuriating in bed for an extra hour or four, sleeping or reading. It's part of recharging my battery, and my husband is thrilled to accommodate me. In turn I make it possible for him to have his long afternoon naps.

Taking back my mornings was transformative, and I can't recommend it enough. It's like putting on your oxygen mask on an airplane before helping others. It's not a selfish indulgence; it's serving yourself before you have to start serving others.

GET ENOUGH SLEEP

Isn't it a little batshit crazy that many of us moms stay up super late every night and consistently feel like crap the next day, but we keep doing this to ourselves because it's the only peace and quiet we get? That's what I did for the first six years that I was a mom. I'd hang on until the delicious stillness in the house set in, when "me time" could start. Granted, me time would often revolve around work, but it was blissfully uninterrupted work. Part of the issue was that I had no stillness in my day. None. More on this later. And the other issue was I still had too many Shoulds and Hates on my plate, which made it seem like I had to stay up late to get my work done and time to myself. I'm naturally a night owl, so staying up late wasn't hard, but sleeping in to get enough shut-eye wasn't possible with kids and a business that touched people across four time zones.

So I powered through the creation of an enormous business and getting both kids into elementary school, operating under a major sleep deficit. But it took its toll.

We all need sleep to boost our immune system, to have the energy to tackle our days and to control our weight. Yet the average night's sleep for men and women is just six and a half hours, according to Fitbit, the company that sells one of the most popular wearable sleep tracking devices and has tracked more than six billion nights of sleep. During start-up mode, I was lucky if I was getting that much.

Sleep deprivation is a risk factor for depression, heart disease, diabetes, Alzheimer's, dying early, and being a crazy, raving bitch. Through the years John would remind me of this after every bout of pushing myself to the brink of exhaustion. I would invariably get sick and not become so pleasant to live with. Even though I was experiencing more and more success, and more opportunities were coming my way, I couldn't enjoy it because I was so effing tired. Kind of ironic that I'm the wife of a doctor whose one of many specialties is sleep, but I still maintained this destructive habit. I finally cried uncle when the pain was too great.

I've known for a long time that I need at least eight hours of sleep to act like a sane and energized human. So if I was going to get some stillness before the kids woke up, I'd have to start going to bed at 10:00 p.m. every night. John pointed out that it also meant I'd have to say good night to my phone, iPad, and laptop by 9:00, since the light emitted from those suckers can significantly decrease our brain's ability to secrete melatonin, a hormone responsible for helping us fall asleep. It's pretty hard to argue with him when he starts citing studies, and I was just too damn tired to put up a fight.

So no later than 9:00 p.m., the laptop and iPad go in my office and my phone automatically goes to Do Not Disturb. If I listen to a book or a podcast on my phone while I'm getting washed up, I have to walk downstairs and leave it in the kitchen to charge or I know I'll be tempted to check YouTube to see the latest from Stephen Colbert or Trevor Noah, and then see what I've missed on Instagram and then check email just one more time.

If I've got any energy left, I read for a few minutes, and then I grab my journal to jot down at least three things I'm grateful for that happened during the day. I make sure to end the day just as I began it—focusing on the positive. Or if both of us have energy left, we get lucky before I journal, which usually makes it onto the gratitude list.

Please understand that I didn't flip a switch one day and all of a sudden had a perfected habit in place. Just like getting up early, my routine for getting enough sleep evolved over time. It took a bit of trial and error, adding and revising to come up with the best practices for me to ensure success.

I'm not going to lie: getting to bed early has been the most challenging of all my habits. And I've fallen off the wagon. I'm not talking about staying up late on a Saturday night or while on vacation. I've found that if 90 percent of the time I'm keeping to a solid eight hours of shut-eye, my body can handle the occasional shortfall. But a couple of years ago, when it was a particularly stressful time in our business and one of our kids was going through a rough period, I started reverting to my old sleep habits. And once I broke the healthy habit chain for a week, it turned into months. And when I finally crashed, it was ugly.

A blood test showed that the Epstein-Barr Virus, which I first contracted during a college bout of mono, was back with a vengeance. I was so sick that I could barely function. In addition to tweaking my diet to 95 percent plant-based (that's when the celery juice came in the picture), and following a nutritional supplement regimen John created for me to kill the virus and strengthen my body and immune system, I spent the next three months sleeping, resting, reading, and doing little work.

When I got back on my feet again, I knew I couldn't allow

myself to go into a long-term sleep deficit again. The pain of not being able to live my full and beautiful life was big and scary enough. Now I know that if I really want to stay up past 10:00 p.m., it better be worth it because I will have to sacrifice my treasured morning routine to get in my eight hours. And when I don't— which will likely happen a couple of times in the next month for me to get this book done on time—it won't be for more than a few days at a time. I refuse to deprive my body of the nightly nourishment it so desperately needs to stay healthy. Exhaustion is not a requirement to Have It All. In fact, it could end up being one of the greatest obstacles.

USE MULTIPLIERS INSTEAD OF MULTITASKING

Multitasking has become a badge of honor. The ability for us women to do two or more discrete things at the same time is glorified as the ultimate in efficiency. We text while in a meeting, we read emails while talking to our kids (come on, we've all done it), among a whole host of other tasks we try to accomplish simultaneously as if our brains were a microchip.

But research shows that multitasking isn't nearly as efficient as we all like to believe, and it can even be harmful to our health. Even though we like to think of ourselves as Wonder Woman, our brains actually have a finite amount of attention and productivity. If we're doing two activities at once, then we're never fully "in the zone" for either one of them. And if we're trying to juggle three or more things at once, forget about it. The research shows we won't be doing any of them with excellence.

First off, let's call out the fallacy of the word "multitasking." Scientists have figured out that our brains can think about only one thing at a time, so when we're multitasking, we're really switching back and forth between tasks. And we're not fully present in any of them. We're more likely to make mistakes, and it can make us as much as 40 percent less productive. A decade of research shows multitasking wreaks havoc on our memory. It applies to those who have many media channels open at once, so listen up if you typically have your laptop open, stop to respond to a text, and have the news going on your iPad at the corner of your desk. You're likely to perform significantly worse on simple memory tasks.

I must admit, it wasn't until I read the research that I connected all this task-switching to my increased stress, zapped energy, and inability to remember things. Once I realized how much multitasking was causing these joy-robbing, performance-diminishing issues, I stopped subscribing to the myth that I was being super-efficient and accepted that there was no way I could be superhuman.

How many times have you had a conversation with your spouse or your co-worker while trying to do something on a device, and then you have no recollection of what you talked about? I sure have. How many of us have blamed our diminished memory on "mom brain"? I don't think it's because we have kids. It's that we're multitasking too damn much.

Once I learned that trying to do two or more cognitively taxing things at once was destructive, I started learning about the concept of multipliers and how they could help me accomplish more of what I wanted in life. A multiplier is a single activity that fulfills multiple goals, and because we're only doing one thing, we're fully present (can I get a hallelujah?). Stanford Graduate

School of Business professor Jennifer Aaker advocates creating a single activity and striving to achieve two, three, or four goals at the same time. Like going for a hike with a fellow nonprofit volunteer to talk through fundraising ideas (been there) or having a lunch meeting with takeout while you and your colleague wait for your cars to be washed (done that).

Another perennial goal is consistent date nights with John. Yet with so much on our plates and how much we rely on collaboration to keep all the balls in the air, we make one date a month a "working session" to go over things like helping each other with a business challenge, or to brainstorm vacation ideas, or to make the gift list for the holidays. We still get time alone together, we get a great meal that we didn't cook and there aren't any dishes to do, and we accomplish something that's important to us.

Constantly searching for more multipliers has helped me become what Aaker calls more "time affluent." I've taken her suggestion of constantly asking how I can make an activity a multiplier,especially during my Sunday scheduling meetings with myself. I encourage you to come up with a couple of multipliers you can do in the coming week to see how much time and connection it gives back to you.

There's one exception to the one-thing-at-a-time rule: if you're doing a physical task that you've done over and over. Things like walking, jamming on an elliptical machine, and folding laundry are automatic, so they don't require cognitive thought and free up our brains to focus on something else. It makes sense that it never stresses or tuckers me out to do business calls or listen to personal or professional development during cardio sessions, while washing and cutting fruits and veggies, or while putting away laundry.

Especially once I started working from home, I made the most of every brainless activity I could to meet professional or personal goals. So listening to an audiobook while driving (if you're an experienced driver) is good. Texting while writing an email is bad. Since task-switching can slow us down and make us less effective, I've also gotten increasingly disciplined about grouping like activities together on my schedule. I put my uninterrupted focus on a task that requires a specific mindset, and I stay in the groove until I'm finished. This is why I schedule conference calls back-to-back, I cluster coaching calls, I set aside a chunk of time for writing without interruption. It's also another reason I've learned to put my phone away when I'm with my kids, so I can focus on one thing—them—without interruption and without half-assing work or parenting.

Clearly multitasking is *not* the way to Have It All, but grouping like activities and using multipliers are.

DITCH THE DISTRACTIONS

We live in an age when distractions are bombarding us all the time. Alerts, notifications, texts, rings. We've just gone over what that does to our productivity, our memory, and our sanity. And if you work from home like I do, the distractions multiply thanks to pets, the laundry, workmen, kids, and the refrigerator. If we don't learn to be disciplined about all of it, it can quickly eat up the time we've set aside for the different things we want to tackle on any given day.

In my business, I work with tens of thousands of women who

rely on me for information, and at any one time I can be working closely with as many as fifty of them. Add to that my work with nonprofits, everything my kids are involved with, and all my interests and hobbies, and I have communications of some form coming to me literally every fifteen minutes or less. And I bet you do too. I had to figure out ways to insulate myself from this never-ending onslaught so I could stay in control of my days.

Let's start with technology distractions, because for me it's the most pernicious and destructive diversion, as you'll read in the next chapter. I first had to come to terms with the fact that I don't have to respond to everyone immediately after they contact me. I set aside time specifically reserved for responding to emails: twenty minutes in the morning before getting the kids ready for school, while the kids are doing their homework, and before powering down for the day. Those who work closely with me know that if they need me to respond sooner, they need to text.

But I'm not responding to texts right away either. I put my phone on Do Not Disturb when I'm working on a project, and I won't check notifications unless I'm on my hourly "bust a move" breaks (more on this in a moment). Now, some of you mamas might be panicking as you think about spending much of your day on DND: "What if my child needs something?" Wipe your brow, Sister; technology has our backs. It's possible to designate which of our contacts can bypass this quiet time. On my iPhone, I've marked as favorites John, Nate, our nanny/wife Linda, the kids' school, my assistant, and my mom when she's having health issues. In reality, these are the only people who might have to get in touch with me because of a real emergency. And if it's not an emergency, it can wait for an hour or more.

Unless I'm doing a social media campaign that requires me to respond in real time, I don't check these apps more than four times a day: once in the morning, once midday, once late afternoon, and once at night. These times are designated on my daily schedule because I had to break the addiction to my phone (more on this later). And when I do get on social media, I set a timer on my phone for five or ten minutes (depending on how much I have to do on there). When the timer goes off, I get off and get back to the rest of my life.

I spend a lot of time looking at my laptop, and I found that I had to be as vigilant with it as I am with my phone. I close every program I'm not using to keep me from being distracted from the task at hand. I've also permanently disabled all notifications on my laptop, so I don't have to triumph over the temptation to take a look.

For those of you who work from home, we have a whole bunch of other things enticing us. I stick to my daily schedule, and if it's not on there, I don't do it. Otherwise I'll avoid doing the hard stuff by doing a myriad of things that aren't mission critical. Even when the doorbell rings, if I'm not expecting someone, I don't answer. Because it's not on my schedule. And I've had to train my family that when the door to my office is closed, it means I'm unavailable unless a human or a dog is bleeding or barfing or dying.

There's no doubt that the habits I've adopted to insulate myself from distractions have been essential to my life. It requires discipline, no doubt, but the pain of having one of my precious days on Earth go by without having a hell of a lot to show for it is far too great. The key to these habits has been eliminating the distractions before they have the chance to divert my attention. I figure I have only so much willpower at my disposal on any given day, and so do you. It's so silly to waste it on this nonsense.

GET OFF YOUR ASS

Exercise is so important to me. It not only keeps my insides healthy and keeps me fitting into my clothes, but it also makes me happy. It clears my head, boosts my energy, and brightens my mood on even the most challenging days. But with everything I juggle and the unpredictable nature of motherhood and travel and running a business, I can't get a workout in every day.

I've learned to incorporate habits that cause me to bust a move more, so that on the days I can't fit in a workout, I'm not a sedentary sloth, and I don't feel like a failure.

We've all seen the headlines that proclaim that sitting is the new smoking. And as a writer, I'm sitting on my ass a lot. Add to that the years and years spent as a lawyer and a PR executive sitting in an office for at least eight hours a day. That's a lot of cigarettes. That's why now I stand every chance I get.

When I redecorated my home office, I added a table that's the perfect height for me to stand and work at. My desk is reserved solely for writing projects (I have no idea why, but I don't write as well when I stand), and for everything else—video conferences, emails, social media, and more—I'm usually on my feet.

Phone calls are a big part of my business, and if I don't have to refer to any documents or anything on a screen, I walk and talk around my house, in our backyard, or around the block. I first got in this habit when I started my business, when Bebe was just six months old. One of the only ways I could fit in exercise in those days was pushing her around the neighborhood in her stroller. And since I was still working in public relations, I had to make the most of every spare moment to work what was then my side gig. I monetized our daily strolls in the fresh air, while also chipping away at my baby weight. No wonder some of Bebe's first words were "eye cream" and "peptides." And I found that when I walked and talked, I sounded more energized, and I was more magnetic, which certainly helped with all my calls.

Whether I'm working while standing or sitting, it's easy for me to get engrossed in what I'm doing. So I set my alarm on my phone every hour to prompt me to stop and take a "bust a move" break I previously mentioned. I walk around our house, up and down our stairs, or around the block. It's also a valuable break for my brain and a healthy screen break for my eyes.

I never take escalators when there are stairs. And because I love games, I make a game out of finding the farthest parking spot, even if I'm getting to the school program with two minutes to spare. Speed walking is even better exercise, right? All this movement keeps me from feeling guilty for not getting in a formal workout.

And, more important, it keeps my head clear for all parts of my life, and because I'm keeping my serotonin levels up, I walk around a hell of a lot happier.

CELEBRATE THE LITTLE VICTORIES

My whole life I've had big, hairy, audacious goals. I've learned that if I wait to reward myself until I reach the summit of a mountain, then I'm not treating myself as kindly as I'm treating others. I prize my kids for making incremental advances. I reward my team as they advance along their entrepreneurial journey toward their goals. So why wouldn't I do it for myself? Ever since high school, I've hit goals, wiped my brow, and then started working toward the next one. And while it's comfortable and fun to reward others, it seems unnecessarily indulgent to reward ourselves. What a bunch of bullshit.

I knew I had to get in the habit of taking a minute and celebrating what I've accomplished, no matter how small, because it's how we show ourselves the love we deserve and so easily give to others. I knew it would help train me to Focus on doing the things I've declared are important to me, and it's behavior I want to model for our kids.

Since my business requires me to reach out to people every day, when I've hit my goal five days in a row, I reward myself with a weekly treat that I wouldn't otherwise do for myself. Back when we were operating on a tight family budget, reading a book while drinking a latte from my favorite coffeehouse was an indulgence worth working toward. When I do an organizational project, like cleaning out my closet, I reward myself with indulgent me time. As I've been writing this book, when I hit my daily goal, I get to dig through all my emails for the latest sales from my favorite stores.

Committing to our habits is a victory and deserves rewards, which will increase our belief in our abilities to stay on track, that failure baggage be damned. And several of my successful habits are actually a reward for accomplishing another habit. When I allow myself to grab my beloved coffee twenty minutes after drinking my celery juice, it's a reward for keeping this healthy habit. What's immediately rewarded is significantly more likely to be repeated. We're simple animals, after all.

YOUR HABITS

Now it's your turn to figure out what habits you should add to your life. It's going to require you to get real about your pain points and what you could do to eliminate them. Remember to be specific about what your habit involves and when you'll do it. They don't have to be huge, sweeping changes; they have to start solving one of your pain points and can evolve over time like mine have.

You'll be more likely to commit to your habits if you remember that you don't have to Focus on the whole habit, just the beginning. Mel Robbins's 5-Second Rule, which commands us to count down from five and take action after we get to one, is so powerful because we only have to take action for one second. In his book *Atomic Habits*, habits guru James Clear says, "When you start a new habit, it should take less than two minutes to do." Once you've started doing the action, it's easier to keep doing it. I now understand why my intention to exercise for fifteen minutes can easily extend to thirty minutes once I get going, and my goal of making five work calls easily extends to ten or more once I get in a rhythm.

It's all about, as Clear writes, mastering the habit of showing up. The hardest part is the very first action. When we do that, we're on our way.

PAIN	HABIT TO RELIEVE PAIN	HOW I CAN ENSURE SUCCESS
Not enough energy to keep up with my kids	Work out 30 minutes M. W. Fr before work in my bedroom	Workout clothes next to my bed

You can download a printable version of my Have It All Habits Log at romineustadt.com/resources.

If you're anything like me, you'll have days when you struggle with habits because you're tired or stressed or PMSing or pissed off or just don't feel like it. Focus on the pain you're trying to relieve, and just show up. If you stumble, remember to have grace with yourself, and get right back on the habit horse the next day. Take the time to figure out why you got off track. Like every stumble in life, we owe it to ourselves to Reflect, Revise, and Release. Think about what happened and why, figure out how to tweak what you're doing, and then let go of the slipup. It may be that your habit needs some simple tweaking to help set you up for success. (More about these incredibly powerful three Rs in chapter 10.)

So how long will it take for your new habits to stick? You've likely heard it's twenty-one days to form a habit. But research suggests it takes a lot longer. An often-cited study found it takes, on average, 66 days. But I love what Clear argues. "There is nothing magical about time passing with regard to habit formation. It doesn't matter if it's been twenty-one days or thirty days or three hundred days . . . You need to string together enough successful attempts until the behavior is firmly embedded in your mind and you cross the Habit Line." This means we don't have to wait twenty-one or sixty-six days to consider ourselves trained and successful. What matters is that you're showing up and making progress. Which is all we can ever ask of ourselves.

Seven

TAKE CONTROL OVER TECHNOLOGY

Disconnecting from our technology to reconnect
with ourselves is absolutely essential.

—Arianna Huffington

There are a whole lot of people these days (many of them men) preaching to us about how we need to dramatically limit technology, delete apps, shun social media, and even swear off smartphones altogether. I want to tell these people, in the nicest possible way, to fuck off, because my life is possible thanks to technology.

I met the love of my life online. I've built two businesses in large part because of the power of e-commerce and social media. Technology makes my life easier and more efficient. It helps me communicate with my family and friends and with my team that's spread across the US, Canada, and Australia. It's a source of education and inspiration and entertainment.

Just yesterday, here's what my phone enabled me to do:

Order underwear and a protractor for Bebe

Check the weather forecast

Find a gluten-free, vegan muffin recipe

Order Nate court shoes

Track customer orders

Zoom with a potential team member

Update my to-do list

Review venue proposals for a team event

Figure out when my period is coming

Choose meals from our delivery service

Research whether a movie is appropriate for the kids

Buy movie tickets

Narrow down cabinet choices for our kitchen remodel

Check the news headlines

Make a dinner reservation

Add to our grocery list

Listen to a podcast while on a walk

Book a blowout

Post on Instagram and Facebook

Send attagirl videos to team members I'm coaching

Text

Email

Watch last week's *SNL* cold open

I bet you have a similar list. It's like our phones are an assistant that we get to take with us everywhere. So what's the problem?

Here's the problem, and it's big: while technology is helping us to Have It All, it can steal it all away if we let it. If we're not careful and vigilant, our devices keep us from being present in this life we're building.

I know this to be true. My name is Romi Neustadt, and I'm addicted to my phone.

I consider myself in recovery, but it's really, really hard. Because unlike an alcoholic or drug or sugar addict who can stay completely away from the substance she's addicted to, I can't stay away from my phone. That's why controlling technology—instead of allowing it to control me—has been one of my greatest challenges over the last decade, ever since I purchased my first smartphone.

The problem wasn't that I was going on my phone to do the assistant stuff that makes my life easier and more efficient. I became conditioned to pick up the damn thing whenever I was anxious, bored, nervous, frustrated, tired, or scared to dive into the hard stuff. I know I'm not the only one. Every time I'm in a roomful of other women and the conversation turns to not having enough time, I ask if they think they're spending too much time on the apps on their phones. Their defeated cries of "Hell yes!" prove that the struggle is real for us all. And the shame that comes with succumbing to this addiction, over which we feel powerless, is real too.

Any activity that starts to interfere with our daily life and diverts us from our Priorities is a big red flag waving for our attention. If we're trying to fill our days with the things that are really important to us, but the lure of our phones is keeping us from getting to them, that's a problem. How we spend our days is how we spend our life. When I realized that my life was being lived primarily on my phone, I had to come to terms with the cumulative cost of being at the mercy of those apps.

Once again, it's not about my lacking discipline or an inability to understand the harm being done. It's because I'm addicted to the behavior. But it's not my fault. And it's not yours either. According to researchers, including bestselling author Cal Newport, an associate professor of computer science at Georgetown University, tech companies carefully engineer addictive design features like intermittent positive reinforcement and the drive for social approval, to get us hooked. In Newport's book, *Digital Minimalism*, he shares a 2017 admission by Facebook's founding president, Sean Parker, about the attention engineering implemented by the company:

> The thought process that went into building these applications, Facebook being the first of them, . . . was all about: "How do we consume as much of your time and conscious attention as possible?" And that means that we need to sort of give you a little dopamine hit every once in a while, because someone liked or commented on a photo or a post or whatever.

Look how successful they've been. How many times a day do we grab our phones now instead of sitting in stillness or—gasp—looking at the world around us and connecting with other humans? We stand in line at the grocery store and fill the few minutes of waiting by checking Instagram. We escape the office and our kids to sit quietly with a latte and our thoughts but instead pick up our phones to scroll through whatever we can find. We're out to dinner and go to the bathroom with our best friend, our phone. Did you ever think that we as a society would need to bring our phones to pee? We're so addicted that we can't imagine this basic bodily function without technology along for the ride. Do we think we'll fall in and need to make an emergency call? Of course not. What we're doing is no different from doing lines in the bathroom at a club (which, mind you, I've only seen in movies). We're grabbing a dopamine hit. We're drug addicts.

We may give ourselves points for turning off our ringers or setting our phones facedown at the restaurant or on a conference table. But not so fast with the pat on the back. Research shows that its mere presence is grabbing our attention, whether we realize it or not. In an experiment with more than five hundred undergraduate students, those who left their phones outside the room did better on psychological memory and attention tests. And the research shows that the more we depend on our smartphones to function in our lives, the stronger the pull.

It doesn't surprise me that a turned-off or turned-over but still present phone is called a "desirable detractor." If Bradley Cooper were standing in the conference room, I'd have a harder time focusing my attention on the meeting, even if he weren't talking or singing.

But I refuse to accept that I need to shun technology or that I'm powerless. I truly need my phone to do my work and all the other things I want to accomplish in a day. And I want to use it to be educated and inspired and connected with people I otherwise couldn't be.

So I had to create firm boundaries to stop my phone from controlling me. It's about us dictating when and how and how much we're using technology to get what we really want out of life. It ain't easy, but it's possible, if we're as vigilant as the little bastards are addictive.

For those of us who are modeling behavior for kids, it's imperative that we figure this out, because technology will be even more nonnegotiable in their lives, and they're watching everything we do. We've waited longer than most parents to give Nate and Bebe phones. In fact, for most of seventh grade, Nate was the only one in his class without one. We've explained to the kids that they're on screens enough while doing homework on their laptops and the limited time they get on their iPads for entertainment or to rehearse for musicals or dance recitals. We gave Nate his first phone recently for two reasons. First, he's managing his own schedule, and his ability to set up and calendar his appointments and lessons is teaching him valuable life skills and making him feel more empowered. And second, because his extracurricular activities now have him going all over the city and he's still reliant on others to drive him, it's safer and more efficient for us to be able to text with him.

But before we handed over that phone, John and I put together a contract full of restrictions for him to review and sign. Any violation of the contract gives us the right to take away his phone for as long as we deem appropriate, and we also have the right to amend it at any time. And social media is prohibited until we revisit the topic before his junior year of high school. (After I posted about this on social media, so many self-doubting, nervous, and/or weary parents like us exclaimed "I need this!" and begged me to share. So I created a Phone Use Contract for Kids you can download at romineustadt.com/resources. May it help your family as much as it has helped ours!)

I'm not judging any parent who gave their kid a phone before we did; everyone's work and family situations are different, and peer pressure—whether among kids or parents—can be really hard. We've made the decisions we have because we know how challenging it is to tame technology, and our frontal lobes are completely developed. We're terrified of losing our kids in their phones, just like I've sometimes lost me.

Add to the behavioral addiction what the research shows happens to young brains from too much screen time. Studies show that there are structural and functional changes in the brain, including shrinkage in the area of the brain where "processing" occurs, suggesting we're setting up our kids for difficulties with planning, prioritizing, organizing, and basically getting things done. There's also volume loss in the part of the brain that suppresses socially unacceptable impulses, and another that involves our capacity to develop empathy and compassion for others and to integrate physical cues with emotion. This suggests we're also raising a generation that will be lacking in relationship skills.

How can any of us encourage our kids to sit and daydream, interact more with actual eye contact, observe more, read more, and live more in the real world if we're not modeling it for them?

The American Academy of Pediatrics has tips for parents to help our kids tackle smartphone overuse and addiction. Surely we the parents should be following what we want our kids to do. Even if you don't have kids, these are a great place to start.

Designate device-free locations in your home. We've made the dining room and the bedrooms after a certain time media-free.

Implement device curfews when all devices should be turned off. As I mentioned in the previous chapter, it's at least an hour before we turn in to bed.

Designate device-free times together. In spite of protests, we'll make some road trips screen-free (except for accessing music or audiobooks), museum outings, and even entire trips. Last year for Nate's bar mitzvah celebration in Israel, the kids had to leave their iPads home. They were incredulous, but after the trip they both conceded that they didn't miss them and they were much more "in the moment" and "got more out of it" than if they were trying to get in screen time.

HOW I WENT INTO RECOVERY

I've made every technology mistake out there—from sleeping with my phone next to my bed, to checking it during a meal with a friend or family member, to keeping all the alerts and notifications on, to checking a text while driving (really not proud of that one), and so much more. No matter what kind of a hopeless addict you think you are, you're no worse than I've been. But you have to want to change. Your pain has to be bigger than the pain of changing your behavior. Sound familiar? The pain of what I was missing out on and the pain I'd experience if I knew I contributed to fucking up my kids with horrible modeling were big enough for me. So one by one, I changed my relationship to my phone.

I started using the off button

Hitting Do Not Disturb wasn't too painful, but turning off my phone completely has always been hard for me. In the first several years of my business I told myself that something urgent might need my attention. And I now recognize that my phone was giving me frequent hits of dopamine that were easing the anxiety I felt while in start-up mode. I've since learned that nothing is so urgent that it can't wait a few hours, especially on the weekend. I'm not POTUS, for God's sake.

As moms we tend to tell ourselves that we need to be able to be reached at all times in case our darlings need something. I can allow myself that, even if it is slightly irrational, because I have kids who often end up in the nurse's office. But when my most important peeps—John, Nate, and Bebe—are with me, I've accepted that my phone doesn't have to be on at all times.

A few years ago I started turning it off for chunks of time while having family time at home or on vacation. It was hard at first—even twitch-inducing—but then it got easier and now provides a feeling of relief I actually look forward to. Last summer both our kids were away at their respective sleepaway camps, and outside real-time communication was forbidden. I started turning off my phone for larger chunks of time when the kids weren't with me—even eight hours straight one Sunday! Guess what? I didn't miss anything urgent. And I was present the whole day.

Now I shut it off every week for a few hours on the mornings I get to stay in bed and read. I use my phone to turn on our Sonos system to play music, I snap a picture if I want to share what I'm reading on social, and then I put it in another room. If I don't, it's too easy for me to grab and lose the precious time of self-care.

I set a timer

Some people have to weigh and measure their food to avoid overeating. I have to measure how long I'm on social media or I'll go into a trance, and before I know it, I've lost precious time down the scroll hole. Before I go on the apps, I set my phone timer for either five or ten minutes, depending on how much I have to do on there. And when I get cocky and think I don't have to do so, I invariably find that twenty minutes have disappeared with nothing to show for it.

If I'm going on social media for work, I also write down on a Post-it the discrete tasks I'm going to do. When I'm done with them, I'm off. If something catches my eye but isn't on my list, I take a picture of it or put it in a saved Instagram folder to review as a reward when I've done the stuff on my schedule for the day, but again with a timer set.

I put the damn thing away

Even before I read the research on how our silenced or turned-over phone distracts us, I knew it made me more anxious and was too tempting to grab. So I started putting my phone in my purse when at a restaurant or in a meeting (which, by the way, the research shows is still distracting, but it's better than having it within sight). And in the last year I've noticed that it's still distracting if the people I'm with have theirs out. I now suggest, "How about we all put our phones away?" The only exception is if one or more of us are waiting on an important call that we simply can't miss. And if I have to look at my phone for an essential reason, I force myself to say out loud, "I'm so sorry, but I have to look at my phone, so I'm going to step away for a moment. Please excuse me." Only real emergencies get me to stop the meal or the conversation and walk away.

If the people I've pissed off by looking at my phone while we spent time together are reading this, they're no doubt rolling their eyes and thinking, "Well it's about time you realize how obnoxious you were." All I can say is I'm sorry and ask for grace. Like all addicts, we don't know what awful stuff we're doing until we know.

I say No to notifications

I turn off every alert possible. I don't have live notifications for email or social media, and I decline every app's request to send me them. The only notifications I get are those that are necessary for me to see—like text and an important communications app for my business—but I curb them with the Do Not Disturb setting. This simple practice protects me from a whole lot of things that aren't important.

I carry a book around with me

I keep a book in my car so that I can bring it with me in case I find myself with some free, unscheduled time like waiting for an appointment and grabbing a bite alone. This prevents me from defaulting to scrolling on social, and the less I do it, the less I want to do it. If I can't carry a book, I always have an audiobook going. Yes, it's on my phone, but I activate Do Not Disturb, and my Audible app is the only thing I allow myself to access.

I flushed the bathroom habit

Here's my latest effort to fight my addiction: I'm no longer bringing my phone with me to the bathroom, even when I'm home, so
I eliminate the habitual cue. If I'm unable to separate myself from
my phone while I'm out, I put it in my purse and hang it on the
hook. I leave it at the table of a restaurant whenever possible to
eliminate any need to use willpower. I'm loving being alone with
my thoughts while I go number one, and I'm fitting in more reading when I go number two. Bathroom breaks are now truly a
break.

I learned to take just one photo

Here's another thing that complicates our addictions: most of us
use our phones as a camera. If we leave it home, unless we have
another camera, we won't be able to take any pictures. So it comes
down to how many damn pictures and videos does one person
need to take? And whether we're willing to be disciplined enough
to sometimes confine our phone use to camera only.

You've likely heard the joke that's not so funny anymore: if we
don't post about it, it must not have happened. When did we become a society that documents our lives instead of living them? I
had to make a decision whether I was going to capture everything
for posterity and social media or be present and experience the
wonder of this life I was creating.

An essential part of connecting with my tribes and building
my businesses is showing all parts of my life. But that doesn't

mean I have to share everything I do to be relevant and success-ful. And neither do you.

I've been criticized for not capturing photos, including on those insanely decadent incentive trips we've earned. But it's be-cause I've been so engrossed in the moment and with connecting with other humans in the real world. And I'm done apologizing for it.

Do I regret not having pictures of everything? No. But I sure would've regretted not being all in while frolicking on the grounds of the Althorp Estate, wine tasting in Tuscany, floating in the turquoise lagoon in Bora Bora, or playing with elephants in Thai-land.

How often are we at a concert and are filming it so we can share with everyone on social media? I've actually curbed my dancing so I don't jostle the phone, which is completely ridiculous because I bought the tickets to enjoy dancing to an artist live. How many of us have tried to get a video of our kids' entire pro-gram, play, or recital? Unless we're trying to put together an au-dition reel or need to show a family member who really wants to see it and couldn't be there, is it necessary? I may have captured the performances, but I can't say I really took in these precious moments in the kids' lives.

To stop this madness, I've adopted a One-and-Done Rule. At any event or outing, if I want to capture it—or need to for my work—I take one picture or a short video clip that will give me something to post about and spark a flood of memories when I see it again. There's no doubt I find this hard, most especially with my colleagues at important business events, where I feel pressure to get the perfect shot or the perfect video clip. But I keep remind-ing myself that it's always more important to be present in my life.

IF I CAN DO IT, YOU CAN DO IT

The average person reportedly spends two hours a day on social media. And that doesn't include all the other reasons we go on our phone. There are apps, like Moment, that can tell us just how much time we're spending and where. But I'm less concerned about the amount of time I'm on my phone and more focused on whether that time is productive. I value my professional goals and maximizing convenience and efficiency. I love the core question that Newport says we should be asking ourselves: "Is this the best way to use technology to support this value?" I continue to strive to use my phone to Have It All, but not to fill in the empty spaces, avoid the hard stuff, ease my anxiety, or fight boredom. If you take baby steps to use your technology to support your values instead of working against them, you too can go into recovery.

What are the baby steps you're going to commit to right away to tame technology in your life?

....

....

....

....

....

Now set a calendar reminder (yes, on your phone, if that's where you keep your schedule) for every two weeks to check in with yourself and be honest about how well you've kept your commitment. If you're successfully keeping with the changes, push yourself to add even more Focus to your phone use, questioning if other things you're doing are the best way to support your value that's important to you. If they are not, take more baby steps to change your behavior.

You may find that some changes are not going well because you're simply requiring too much discipline to outmuscle your addiction. Don't get frustrated; just make changes like I've had to do, like leaving the phone out of the room instead of just turning it to DND. There's no shame in slipups; the point is to learn why they're happening and to come up with a strategy to avoid them.

Remember, more beeps, tags, buzzing, and pop-ups don't make us more important or more successful. But they sure can make us feel like our heads are going to explode and make us wildly unproductive. Yes, your phone may be one of your assistants. And that assistant works for you, not the other way around.

The next time you pick up your smartphone, show her who's smarter, and show her who's boss.

Eight

EMBRACE QUIET

*Almost everything will work again if you unplug
it for a few minutes, including you.*

—Anne Lamott

There's another essential piece to this Have It All puzzle
that we must dig into. And it has nothing to do with
doing. It has to do with being.

Being quiet.

We are all inundated with activity, stimuli, and noise coming
from all different places—our TVs, our devices, our families, our
friends, our colleagues, and sometimes it feels like the whole world
is talking at us. My dear friend Holly Brewer describes it perfectly:
"We get surrounded by all that noise, and after a while it feels like
a bunch of chaos. Then if I don't get quiet, it starts to feel like the
chaos is happening inside of me too." A-to-the-men.

I've often been so Focused on being productive that I've moved
quiet time to the back burner, even when I've declared it a Goal
to serve my health Priorities. Because my *doing* has historically

taken precedence over my *being*. Until it couldn't anymore. I learned the hard way that even if we can get to a Have-It-All life without quiet, it's pretty impossible to stay there. And I've got scientific and some pretty damn compelling anecdotal proof to convince you.

SCIENTIFIC PROOF FOR QUIET

Science tells us that our brains won't sustain nonstop high-level performance indefinitely.

We need blank spaces in the day when our brains are doing nothing so they can get a much-needed rest. The ceaseless demands of our modern lives, with all these decisions and disruptions and things to do, put a major burden on the prefrontal cortex of our brains. According to brain experts, when we don't give our noggins a break, our "attention resources" get depleted. Which is why we feel mentally fried, making it hard for us to solve problems, come up with new ideas, deal with stress and to Focus.

But it doesn't have to be this way. According to "attention restoration theory," our brains can restore their cognitive resources when we reduce all that noise coming in. Research shows that silence can even grow our brains. A 2015 study on mice found that periods of daily silence led to new cells developing in the hippocampus, a key brain region for learning, memory, and emotion. And the quieter we are, the better. A 2006 study that measured changes in blood pressure and blood circulation in the brain found that just two minutes without stimuli coming in is more relaxing than longer periods listening to "relaxing music."

Clearly the science is compelling that we have to spend some time every day Focusing on not focusing. But it's not just about shutting out all the noise to take care of our brains. We need quiet to hear the most important voice of all—our own. The voice inside all of us that wants to guide us, alert us, warn us, and calm us. Call it what you want—your gut, your subconscious, your inner guru. I call it the Heart Voice. It's oh so wise and helpful.

But here's the thing: we've got to be able to actually hear it. And in our modern lives of constant alerts and media and co-workers and planning committees and opinions and kids and pets and our calendars and to-do lists, our Heart Voice that's trying to talk to us gets drowned out.

YES, YOU HAVE TIME FOR QUIET

I completely understand if you're thinking, "This makes sense, but how the eff am I supposed to find quiet time every day?" If your health is one of your Priorities (which I hope it always is), and it's undeniable that our brains need quiet to be healthy, then make time for it you must. Stick with me, because it's not a daunting proposition once you understand what quiet time requires and what it doesn't.

Remember part of the great news: the research brainiacs (pun intended) found that long periods of quiet aren't necessary to reap the benefits. As you delegate or delete the Hates and Shoulds from your life, as well as tame your tech addiction, I promise that you can find little pockets for this necessary self-care. And let's tell ourselves a different story, shall we? Instead of "Ugh, I *have* to fit in some quiet time," you flip it to "I *get to* have some quiet now. Yay!"

QUIET DOESN'T REQUIRE STILLNESS

I think it's easy to confuse quiet and stillness and assume that in order to experience health-benefiting, Heart Voice–enabling quiet, we've got to be physically still. It's about turning off what's coming into our ears and, ultimately, our brains. For many of us, we can reap the benefits of quiet while in motion.

Marissa McDonough is mom to three girls who are as dynamic as their mama. She's also an entrepreneur, a speaker, a real estate investor, and one half of a powerful and loving partnership with her husband, Roger. I often joke with her that she does more in a day than most people do in a month, and she responds with some variation of "It takes one to know one," or "Shut up, you're just as nuts as I am." Maybe it's our Butte, Montana, roots or that we both simply have so much we want to do while we're alive on Earth. Either way, Marissa (aka "Riss") is as balls-to-the-walls as I am, and I love her like a sister.

Because of how many things she has her hands in, Riss has an insane amount of noise coming in every day. She's learned that "quiet time is not optional. It grounds me and keeps me from being reactive and lets me tap into how I'm feeling and what I really want."

Her daily go-to is walking her golden retriever, Gus, when the weather's good or cross-country skiing in her neighborhood with her pup in tow during the often long yet beautiful winters under the Big Sky. By combining quiet with the time outdoors she craves and the exercise she knows she and Gus need, she's more likely to make it happen.

Since she's often trying to fit in as much as possible in a day, Riss still sometimes makes the mistake of thinking she can multitask quiet time. "Because there's so much on my plate, it's easy for me to think that my walks or ski time also has to serve as my personal development time, and I'll throw on a podcast or listen to a book," she said. "But that's not quiet; it's more noise coming in. And I don't get the benefit I need.

"Because I deal with people all the time, I've learned that if I don't have quiet—no people, no talking in my head—I get to the point where I hate people," Riss admitted with a laugh. "Which is clearly not good for any part of my life or who I want to be."

My friend and fellow school mom Daniela Jinich finds her quiet through yoga. She has three kids—her twins are in the same grade as Bebe, and her oldest goes to school with Nate. And except for a short period after her twins were born, Daniela has worked nonstop, first as an architect and then as the owner of a successful clothing boutique in La Jolla, California.

A constant throughout the years has been her commitment to a daily yoga practice to "check in with myself and check how my energy level is, how comfortable I am in my body, if there is anything causing too much noise, if I have any energy stuck somewhere that needs to be addressed and so on," Daniela explained. "Our body is a reflection of what's going on in our head that if you pay attention, it will give you a lot of insight into how you're doing emotionally."

Because she's constantly checking in with herself, it didn't take her long to diagnose how the stress from her boutique was affecting her emotional and physical state, which ultimately led her to decide that she wanted to close the doors after seven years in business. And instead of jumping right into another endeavor, this workhorse is committed to enjoying plenty of quiet time so she can figure out what she wants to do next. She just returned from the weeklong yoga retreat she does at least once a year. All outside stimuli are banned, which she finds is the ultimate check-in with herself. And she's hiking and spending lots of time in nature.

"It's helping me focus on what's important to me, setting my priorities and treating myself nicely. It's giving me the opportunity to hold space for myself and giving me energy to be able to hold space for my three kids," Daniela said. "And when the time is right, I'll know what I'm supposed to do next."

My aforementioned dear friend Holly loves running—not inside on a treadmill but in the beautiful North Carolina outdoors or anywhere that work and play takes her. Throughout raising her now college-age older son and her teen younger son, and growing her own large skincare business, Holly has made daily runs nonnegotiable because it's where some of her greatest quiet happens.

"I figured out years ago that when my body is busy doing a mundane task—like running or washing dishes—my mind becomes still," Holly said. "When I think about it, some of the best and most important decisions I've made—to get married, planning our family and how we'd raise our children, my career choices—have happened while on a run. I don't listen to music; I'm out in nature, and all I can hear is the pitter-patter of my feet. That's what creates the mental and spiritual stillness for me to get clarity."

QUIET DOESN'T HAVE TO MEAN NOT TALKING

The other way Holly gets enough quiet to hear the voice inside her is by talking. Not to a person in the physical world but to a higher power. "This has served me through my adult life, and it stems from a place of believing in something bigger than me, a divine presence in my life who is well aware of what's happening inside and outside of me and is intimately concerned with me."

Holly communicates every day with her "Creator"—eyes open, speaking out loud when she's at home by herself and in her head when she's not ("I mean, I don't want to look like a crazy person!"). It's her version of prayer, and it can happen anytime, anywhere. She credits this ongoing conversation with shutting out all the noise so she can get out of her own way and hear what she's supposed to do. "It's how I find the still place inside of me."

WHY THE SHIT HITS THE FAN

When we don't allow for quiet, our whispering Heart Voice becomes louder and louder. And then when we still can't or don't or won't listen, life will throw us a big curveball that *makes* us stop and listen. And along with a little bit of "I told you so," it lovingly helps us make the changes we need to make. Riss, Holly, and I have learned this the hard way.

A few years ago, the proverbial shit hit the fan in one of Riss's businesses and in some of her close friendships. She was so consumed with surviving the professional and personal tornado, her days filled with so much *doing*, she didn't have any time in her day for quietly *being*. "And because I wasn't being quiet, I felt like I was out of control on a hamster wheel, and I couldn't catch my breath. I know everything seemed worse than it was, and I was reacting to things I shouldn't have because I had lost my grounding."

Riss found her quiet that summer sitting in the backyard of her second home on Hauser Lake in Montana, while her youngest napped and her older two played in their clubhouse. "When I let myself stare into that water—there's really something magical about water for me—I was able to hear what the problem was. I figured out that I had been focusing on all the wrong stuff, and it was time to focus on what was really important to me, personally and professionally."

During a particularly crazy-busy time for Holly—business in hyper-growth, preparing for a big presentation at a conference, building her dream house, and her kids finishing up the school year in what many moms refer to as May-hem—she stopped taking the time for her runs and wasn't having daily chats with her Creator. Her husband, Paul, told her she needed to take it easy, but like many of us who are caught up in periods of high stress and high excitement, we tell others and ourselves that we'll take it easy after we finish just one more thing, and then one more thing. Apparently, her body couldn't wait that long. On Mother's Day that year, things blew up. And by things, I mean her face.

Holly woke up with horrible digestive issues. She hit the Pepto-Bismol, which caused an aggressive allergic reaction. She broke out in a rash all over her body, her face and lips swelled up "like someone filled them with an air hose," and she spent her day in the ER getting two EpiPens.

"It's clear to me and Paul that I got so sick because I wasn't getting the physical rest I needed," Holly said. "I was so caught up in everything I was doing that I forgot to get mental rest. The mental rest would've told me that I needed the physical rest. It sure was telling me then that I needed to say no, that I needed to walk away from some things, that I needed the quiet."

The shit hit the fan for me after running too hard for too long without taking the time to check in with myself. I shot out of the holidays in 2018 making shizz happen. I was armed with my established Priorities and moved at full speed toward my Goals. Then in February I was having lunch with a friend and said, "I'm so incredibly tired. If I could just get sick—not life-threatening sick, but sick enough where I was forced to stop doing everything, and everyone could just leave me alone for a while and I could crawl into bed and sleep. For weeks."

For a type A doer who loves what she does and who she does it with, who loves her children and being a mom, who adores her husband and the endless ideas for projects and travels we banter about, this was *not normal*. Who wishes they were sick? Especially with friends diagnosed and dying from cancer.

This declaration freaked me out so much that the next day I traded my personal development reading time to simply sit in the backyard. I remember thinking that maybe if I sat quietly I'd be able to figure out why I was so tired.

I thought about the past several months and heard the truth as the reality of the last year played in my head. For most of 2017, I had felt like I was dragging myself through my days. Like a cell phone battery that just couldn't fully charge. No matter how much sleep I got, it wasn't enough. No matter how healthy I thought I was eating, it didn't matter. I would feel depleted after my workouts instead of energized. I got every cold or virus that landed within five miles of our house, and I got it worse than everyone else. And I had become a coffeeholic just to get through the day.

My Heart Voice told me that something was wrong, and figuring out what it was had to move to the top of my to-do list, stat.

I went to John that night and confessed how crappy I'd been feeling for so long. And in case you're wondering, not even a brilliant doctor husband is able to recognize health issues when his top-performing wife is so good at ignoring and masking how crummy she's feeling. I ticked off the symptoms I had been powering through: fatigue, headaches and nausea, chills and heart palpitations, achy joints and muscles, and unrelenting brain fog.

John was pretty sure what was going on, and he confirmed it with a thorough run of blood tests. Turns out I was sick. Really sick. Sick as OMFG-I-can't-believe-I've-been-functioning-in-my-life-like-this-sick. Not life-threatening sick, but sick enough where I had to Stop, Drop, and Rest. Not after the next project was completed, or when my mom was fully healed from a surgery, or when Bebe's dance competition season was over. Now.

My test results showed my Epstein-Barr Virus (EBV) was active again and with a vengeance. As I mentioned earlier, I had mono in college, and EBV (the cause of mono, among other things) stays in a body forever, dormant until something weakens our immune system. Since the virus markers were crazy high, I was forced to make my health my top, nonnegotiable Priority, with a slew of supplements prescribed by John and big dietary changes inspired by the book *Medical Medium* and the documentary *What the Health*. I committed to lots of bed rest and only doing the things that I knew I had the energy for, which wasn't much.

In a tearful video I told our team what was going on and that I needed to go dark for a while. I put this book proposal on hold. I declined interviews and speaking engagements. I missed some of the kids' activities and board meetings and social events. And John and I pulled out of a community service trip we'd looked forward to for a year. For four weeks I slept in, took long naps, read books, and introduced myself to Netflix and a predominantly plant-based diet. Some days my biggest accomplishments were making a juice and a smoothie and taking a shower.

Over the course of a month, I had more quiet than I ever remember having in my whole life.

Plenty of quiet time to ponder how I had come to crash so hard. The answer came to me through my Heart Voice screaming, "ENOUGH!" Enough of trying to be all things to all people. Of trying to do and be what others expect me to do. Of taking ownership of others' happiness and well-being. And even though I had been preaching and coaching for years that we should stop Should-ing all over the place, I still had too many of them in my life. Those pernicious little bastards.

In between the naps and celery-juice making and catching up on years of missed TV, I revisited my Priorities and Goals with a clearer vision of what I wanted and needed now, cleaning out tasks, people, commitments, and expectations that were no longer serving me. This was the most important kind of spring cleaning I could ever do. Taking the time once again to clean up my life would not only lead me back to health but help me stay there.

I moved my health to the very top of my Priorities indefinitely, easing back to normal life over the course of several months. But I still haven't returned to full-speed (or what some would call warp-speed) Romi. Not because I can't muster the muscle and grit but because I don't want to live that way anymore. It doesn't serve my Priorities and Goals, and it's not worth the cost.

Here's the ironic part of it all, and why I now knowingly giggle whenever someone tells me they don't have time for quiet: because I didn't regularly incorporate quiet into my life so that I could hear the whispers when my health was starting to decline, I ended up having to spend a hell of a lot more time checked out of my regular life.

Will the EBV flare up again? It will if my Priorities get out of whack again. When I think of the virus, I think of a quote by Tibetan Buddhist nun Pema Chödrön: "Nothing ever goes away until it has taught us what we need to know." For now I'm getting quiet and listening, and I'm making sure that taking care of myself comes first. Because it has to or everything else goes to shit.

FINALLY FINDING MY QUIET

After my big crash of 2018, I was determined to create a quiet practice I would stick to. And I knew it wasn't going to be meditation. If it works for you, God bless you. But after several years of unsuccessful attempts to develop a consistent practice, I considered myself a meditation failure. I joined Oprah and Deepak on their twenty-one-day meditation experiences, not once ever going ten days in a row. I loved the Oprah part, but then Deepak would make me sleepy, and by the time he was done talking, I couldn't remember the Sanskrit mantra of the day he had just told me to recite and I'd fall asleep. I've taken classes that left me antsy and counting the minutes until they were over. I downloaded a slew of apps, and while all these guided meditations are top-notch and many people swear by them, I never became a committed user, staying stuck as a once-in-a-whiler. The huge turning point was when I figured out what meditation could be for me. During that month of rest when I was sick, I'd lay there in bed and focus on my breathing. I found it calming and comforting, and as I recovered and added more activities to my days, I kept it up. Before I knew it, I had settled into a daily practice that felt more like what I thought meditation would be than anything else I had ever tried.

I wasn't trying to stop my thoughts. I was simply letting them flow without judgment. I wasn't trying to quiet my mind. I was simply being quiet. I didn't have to listen to something or someone to guide me through it. I just had to Focus on my breath. I decided upon a minimum of ten minutes a day, because five didn't seem like enough and fifteen felt like it might be too much to fit in some days and keep me from doing it.

I didn't add any other rules to my practice, because Lord knows I have enough rules in my life as it is. I didn't miss the consecutive days of practice the apps would show me, because I have a life filled with enough quantitative goals (monthly revenue, book sales, social media followers). My ten minutes of quiet could happen whenever I felt like I needed it, wherever I was. Turns out this totally chill, just-breathe practice was something I could commit to. And commit I have, for more than a year. I've sat quietly all over my house and in our backyard, countless cars, airports, airplanes, movie theaters, restaurants, and backstage before I speak. I find it amazing that the more I've practiced getting quiet, the less it matters how noisy it is around me.

I love that my meditation practice doesn't require my phone except for the timer, because as you know, I'm an addict. I love that the only thing I have to do is to keep my mouth shut and keep breathing, which I would do anyway, so the odds of being successful here are pretty damn good. If I miss a day, I don't beat myself up. I approach it like all my other habits and simply don't allow myself two missed days in a row.

Since there are so few rules, it never feels like something else on my to-do list. It feels like a treat that I don't want to miss. A grown-up time-out that feels like I'm hitting the reset button on my brain so it can function better. So I can function better. And so I can hear what my Heart Voice needs to tell me. Since I'm listening so often, it only needs to whisper instead of yell.

I've come to rely on this practice most when I need to transition to different parts of my day. For example, this morning was particularly hectic getting the kids off to school. When it came time for me to sit down and write, I felt scattered from rushing to get the kids out the door on time. So it made perfect sense to take ten minutes to sit in silence and breathe. I started my work ten minutes later but was exponentially more productive because I had hit my pause button.

I've found this practice to be so powerful that I'll often take the time to do it more than once a day, even if the second and third times are just five minutes. Before a big meeting or a video shoot, I'll sit still and breathe to center and calm myself so I can be my most effective. When I feel totally spent from the day and I'm not sure if I can possibly go to a social event I've committed to, after five minutes to myself breathing in silence, I'm good to go. And, most frequently, I use this practice when I've been a nonstop #ladyboss all day and have to switch gears to be an all-in mom. I've come to rely on those five minutes to exhale any stress, anxiety, and frustration and inhale calm, peace, kindness, presence—all the good stuff I want to give to my kids.

Maybe you're an expert at some kind of meditation, and if you are, I'm high-fiving you; know that you're better for it. Or maybe you're like I was and have had a love/hate, I-suck-at-this relationship with it. If it's the latter, I implore you to try it again, in a different way. If the apps don't work for you, try my approach without a lot of rules or pressure. Just breathe.

When was the last time you were quiet? Sleeping doesn't count. I'm talking about being alone with your thoughts without any other stimulus coming in. That means reading, listening to audiobooks or podcasts, or watching movies doesn't count either. If it's not happening at all or not often enough, you won't hear your Heart Voice.

I challenge you to clean out the noise so you can hear it. There's no right way to get quiet, and it doesn't have to consume a lot of your time. And although there are some people who don't get quiet because they're afraid of what they might hear—like their Heart Voice telling them they have to make hard and scary changes—don't let that be you. It won't let you ignore it forever, and it's a lot easier to respond to whispers than to screams for help.

Nine

MAKE
AUTHENTICITY
NONNEGOTIABLE

Let go of who you think you're supposed to be;
embrace who you are.

—Brené Brown

Everyone's talking about authenticity these days, and before you roll your eyes that I'm about to become one of them, slow your roll. Everyone's talking about it because it's that important. And not enough of us are doing it.

Trying to be someone other than our true self is exhausting. And here's the real conundrum and why I'm devoting a whole chapter to this topic: If we're not living as the real us, how can we ever know what we really want out of life? How can we ever determine where we should Focus our time, effort, energy, and emotions? Even if we do know these things, we'll never be able to do them because we won't be nearly as effective, and we'll be exhausted from acting through our lives instead of living them. Trying to be someone other than our true self keeps us from discovering our true north. And it can drain the life-force right out of us. I know from experience.

But living an authentic life is scary. It takes profound courage to be the real us because it forces us to be vulnerable. This is such a big scary thing that Brené Brown has devoted her entire career to exploring just how hard it is and to helping us do it.

A lot of people—myself included—grapple with being authentic because we walk around feeling like a fraud, scared shitless that someone's going to figure out we don't know what we're doing most of the time. We must be a fraud, because c'mon, who are we to think we have anything of value to offer or that we can actually achieve [fill in the blank with your dreams and desires]?

Aren't you tired of trying to be someone else—someone you're comparing yourself to or being compared to? Imagine what you could do if you let the real, powerful you have a chance to come out and play.

I'm telling you, the more I lived my truth, the more authentic I allowed myself to be, the better and better my life got.

But before we talk about my evolution in authenticity and what you can learn from it, let's make sure we're all on the same page here. What exactly does that often thrown-about word "authenticity" mean? To me, authenticity requires us to live in concert (not conflict) with our beliefs and values, not some of the time but all of the time. When we're living in authenticity, what we reveal to the outer world matches what we feel on the inside. It's being ourselves in all parts of our lives, instead of playing a role of what we should be or have been told we should be. (Ah, yes, that damn "S" word again.)

Here's some great news: we all have the ability to live in authenticity. I heaved a sigh of relief when I read what Brené wrote in *The Gifts of Imperfection: Let Go of Who You Think You're Supposed to Be and Embrace Who You Are*:

> It's a practice—a conscious choice of how we want to live. Authenticity is actually a collection of choices that we have to make every day. It's about the choice to show up and be real. The choice to be honest. The choice to let our true selves be seen.

AN EVOLUTION IN AUTHENTICITY

When we start expressing and embracing all the things that make up the real us, that's when our inner power shows up. We can only see our true selves when we let others see us too. And when we do that, lots of incredible magic can happen. It did for me.

I guess you could say my entire adult life has been a constant battle—or dance, if you're a glass-half-full kind of girl like me—between living an authentic life and spending so much time, effort, and energy to be who I thought I was supposed to be. As Brené says, authenticity isn't a switch we can turn on and off; it's an evolution fueled by little and big decisions every day. I'm grateful that each time I chose the real me, it taught me how to recognize when I found myself at a crossroads and how to allow authenticity to win (or lead). I'm also grateful for the people placed into my life at many of these important crossroads who challenged me by asking the right questions, like "Is this what I really want? Is this who I really am?" I hope I end up being one of those people for you.

I can trace my struggles with choosing authenticity over expectations (or perceived ones) as far back as my decision to change my college major. Then trading my journalist dreams for the safety of a law degree, to leaving a career as a lawyer that definitely didn't feed my soul. By the time I met John in the early days of online dating (thank you, Jdate.com), I had flexed my authenticity muscle enough to allow myself to fall in love with the complete opposite of every guy I ever dated who didn't come in the package I was raised to look for because he felt like home. It was my first e-commerce success story.

But the biggest tests of my commitment to authenticity were ahead, because the older you get, the more you create, the more you have to lose, the bigger the stakes. By the time I was thirty-eight, we had two babies, and John was busy building a medical practice. I was tired of my second career that was tied to the billable hour, and I was tired of hitting my head against an earnings glass ceiling in PR. I wanted a new adventure, one that would pay me my worth and allow me to be a present, hands-on mom. That's when the chance to join a skincare direct sales company landed in my lap. Direct sales? Me? A UVA Law grad and PR exec and Rhodes scholar finalist? Does someone like me do something like that?

Here I was again, standing at a crossroads, staring at the safe and expected route to my left and the intriguing and exciting unknown to my right. This time the challenging voice came from my husband. "Why do you care what people think? You have to do this, or you'll always wonder what if. What's the worst that could happen?"

"It'll be a flop," I answered.

"Nope," he countered. "The worst thing that will happen is that you'll learn something." I got a good one, didn't I? And learn I did. Things like how much I hate being an employee and how much I love running my own show. That I'm an entrepreneur at heart and adore building something from nothing. What I love most is building communities and building up people, which is really what direct sales is all about.

These last ten years of growing this enormous business have been an exercise in many things. Chief among them has been leaning into my authenticity. I've found myself at a never-ending string of crossroads that have forced me to ask, "What's important to me? What do I stand for?"

I was the first one in my company to coach a minimum standard of excellence that doubled what the company required. "Who does she think she is?" asked the critics. I still knew little about this business model, but I knew enough about me to know that I wanted to coach not to minimums but to the grandest vision of what this could be and what each of us could do with it. And the people who had come to play full out reached for it and kept reaching for every elevated goal I put in front of them. The fact that I was hitting or exceeding everything I coached them to do didn't hurt either.

Less than a year into my business I started doing weekly trainings via conference call, and I still produce an audio broadcast every week for my team that's scattered across the US, Canada, and Australia. The more comfortable and confident I became with what I was coaching, the more I allowed the real me to come through. My sense of humor, a "damn" here and a "shit" there, along with a few f-bombs when appropriate. Although I received emails from team members who expressed concern about my language and others who were downright "appalled," I knew that if I was going to make it through this entrepreneurial marathon, I could only do it as an unapologetic, uncensored me. I told my critics that I knew I wasn't everyone's cup of tea and that I wouldn't be offended if they plugged into other accomplished business leaders for training and inspiration.

My team continued to grow at a staggering rate, and my trainings attracted thousands of business builders from around the company who weren't even on my team. I became known as the no-BS straight shooter you could count on to tell you how to build this sucker, with humor and a little ass-kicking thrown in, and yes, a few choice four-letter words. I still wasn't everyone's cup of tea, but for those who liked what I was serving up, I was hitting the spot. The more I kept doing me, the bigger we grew.

I was loving my gig, and loving being myself. Yet when I was asked to appear in the company's early success-story videos, the corporate execs with whom I had a mutual love affair off-camera weren't digging me on-camera. I spent two agonizing shoots where I was told to "be less Romi" and "tone down the energy." It was frustrating to be told to tone down the very things that earned me a spot in the videos to begin with. To be less Romi is not to be Romi at all. I felt like an impostor again—this time on a real set—trying to play someone other than me. My performances were flat, and I vowed that I'd never again agree to be anything other than me, even if it meant I didn't participate. Now I'm one of the go-tos when they need to crank out a quick video because I can give them what they need in my own unique style in just one or two takes. And I get thousands of views of my social media videos sharing tools and inspiration, all while being completely Romi.

But don't think that once you learn to flex your authenticity muscle that you'll never find yourself at a crossroads again. This battle (or dance) is for life. And it can be harder to be true to yourself when it feels like everybody's watching.

It was scary as hell to write my first book, not just because I didn't know if people would like it or think it was helpful and inspiring. But also because I had a whole lot to say, and I was going to say it in my unfiltered, authentic voice. It's one thing to be unabashedly you when talking, but it's a whole other thing when you commit it to the printed page, where it will be around forever. And then it came time to choose a title, which I find is the hardest part of writing a book.

After coming up with nothing the least bit fantastic, I asked my business partner and former agency colleague, Bridget Cavanaugh, to come up with a title. Bridget is one of my favorite people on the planet and one of the most brilliant marketing minds I've ever known. Her list of options didn't disappoint. *Get Over Your Damn Self* was her favorite and mine. "You've actually said that before, Romi," she said. "It's so *you*." The rest of the title was easy— *The No-BS Blueprint to Building a Life-Changing Business—* because that's exactly what I had written.

I loved it, but I was nervous. Although I never thought of "damn" as profanity, those early critics of my trainings educated me otherwise. I asked a broad spectrum of friends, colleagues, and experts in the profession for their opinion, including my devout Christian friends.

Everyone liked the title, but several people I respect and admire thought it could alienate some people and warned me not to risk it. After taking in all the opinions, I got really quiet so I could listen to my truth. I channeled my inner Brené to remind myself that authenticity is about sharing on the outside what's on the inside. And inside my book was the unfiltered me.

The response to the book, the title, and everything inside still blows me away. It sold out on Amazon in the first half hour and stayed at number one in several Amazon categories and an Audible category for more than two years. The title was a huge part of sparking the trending #getoveryourdamnself, book clubs, countless pics of my book that still appear on social media nearly every single day. And the most religious among my colleagues are some of the book's biggest fans. A leader of a huge team in our company, who calls herself a "prudish Christian," makes my book part of her team training. She told me, "I would never say the things you do, but I love that you say them." Amen to that.

It's when I had the courage to be my most real that the greatest things in my life happened. I've built an eight-figure business and another career as an author and speaker. And I found the Love of My Life. All because I had the guts to be completely, unapologetically me.

While I treasure each time someone tells me how I've helped them grow their business or grow as a person, the most touching compliments I get are some variations of "You're so real!" and "You're the same down-to-earth person you were before." I believe money and success make you more of who you are, and I'm proud of the hard, courageous work I've done to evolve into more of the real me. Because it's allowed me to serve the people who like what I put out in the world. F-bombs and all.

I kept finding the courage to step into my truth and found my purpose, my people, my joy. I found the best of me. I want you to find the best of you by uncompromisingly and unapologetically being you.

HOW THE COMPARISON GAME EFFS UP AUTHENTICITY

If you haven't been living your truth and going after what you really desire for your life, I bet part of the reason is because you're comparing yourself to others and feeling oh so less than.

We're all playing the comparison game, both online and in the real world. As bad as it was when I was trying to figure out what to major in or what profession to pursue, it's a gazillion times worse now that we can watch what the other gazillion people on the planet are doing at any given moment. Or, at least, what they want us to think they're doing. How does my life, blowout, lunch, kitchen, arm definition, ability to balance my toddler on one hip and hold the hand of my other kid while looking fabulous and rested and not about to lose my shit, measure up to everyone else's? Not so good, amirite?

What I've personally found—and my women friends have confirmed—is that we're more likely to compare ourselves to others when we're unhappy with ourselves or insecure with our choices. And even when we figure out what we really want out of life and what to Focus our time on to get it, if we stay caught up in the comparison game, we'll be too crippled by feelings of inadequacy to go get it.

My dear friend Bridget, the one who named my first book, almost missed out on one of the biggest joys of her life—her new passion of reining—because she was comparing herself to what she thought a rider should look like. Reining is a Western riding competition where the riders guide their horses through a precise pattern of circles, spins, and stops that are judged on precision, smoothness, and finesse. When done well, it's a beautiful and seemingly effortless dance between horse and human.

Bridget has enjoyed a lifelong love affair with horses, and a couple of years ago, after turning fifty, she decided to embark on this challenging new world of reining after finding her beloved horse Watson. I've been in awe of her commitment to this incredibly difficult sport and so proud of her strides at the competitions. If you're a horse person (clearly I'm not, and not even sure that's the right term, but you get the idea), you should follow her on social media because she shares what this sport and Watson are teaching her about herself and life.

But Bridget admits that the biggest hurdle she's had to overcome in the sport isn't technique or being one with Watson. It's that she thought she looked ridiculous in the arena and couldn't be a top rider because she topped the scales. "When I see myself in pictures," she shared on Facebook, "the first word that comes to mind is 'blob.'"

"It's hard in this perfect social media world we live in to be a size 14 on full display in four-color high res images," Bridget confided. "I want to share all these awesome photos of me and Watson, but if you notice, most are from the shoulders up. I crop them to keep the real me out of view."

In her post last January that featured a photo of her in full glory atop Watson, Bridget declared "no more" in service to **Worthy**, her One Word for the year.

"So, from here on out, I'm going to quit making the biggest mistake and that's to feel less than because I'm bigger than. I'm going to try to be my best at any size, in every size and love myself no matter what stares back at me in the photo," she wrote. "My belt is an XL and so are my shirts, but so is my heart too... and that has to count for something."

I've loved watching her post more pictures and videos of her whole self in action, while reining in other parts of her life. Even more, I love that she's allowing herself to feel all the joy Watson and the sport gives her. And by the way, Bridget, your XL heart counts for everything.

I fear that what we're creating for future generations is a standard for what success and fulfillment looks like. And that women will think that in order to be happy you'll have to be a perfect-in-every-way creature who looks a certain way, sports the right accessories, and has all her shit together, all the time. For every Glennon Doyle and Pink and Rachel Hollis—who share their real, their tender underbellies, and their messy—are exponentially more who don't. And it's not just the young and impressionable who are measuring themselves against this carefully curated collection of Insta-perfection. It's women of all ages—grown-up women—and this comparison game is making us feel horrible about ourselves and keeping us from thinking we can have everything out of this life that we want.

If you're comparing yourself to others, stop it. Because whether you realize it or not, it's causing you to hold back on your life. What aren't you doing because you don't look or sound like someone else? Or because you think it's so much easier for another person? Or because everyone else has their act together but you? What a waste. And frankly, what a steaming pile of bullshit you're telling yourself.

Remember, none of us knows what it's really like in someone else's life. I recently wrote a blog about all the struggles we'd had with our strong-willed daughter and the great strides she'd recently made (after I got her permission, of course). I wanted to send an encouraging message to all the parents out there struggling and sad and not knowing if things will change. I also wanted to remind them that there's no shame in getting the help they or their kids need.

After reading 250 social media comments and countless direct messages, three things were clear. First, there are a lot more parents out there struggling with their kids than I knew. That made me feel less alone, and I know it made the others who saw the conversation feel less alone too.

Second, even though I think I share a lot about the good, the bad, and the ugly, people still assume that if you're successful, your life is perfect. "Your family always seems so AWESOME," a fellow entrepreneur wrote. "To hear that there are problems doesn't make me happy, but it reminds me that everyone has stuff they're dealing with. You're still successful through it all, and that is comforting."

And third, people are craving authenticity because it's becoming scarce. In fact, I think we may have reached a tipping point where perfection is actually starting to repel folks instead of attracting them.

OUR AUTHENTIC SELVES WILL ATTRACT MORE OF WHO AND WHAT WE WANT TO ATTRACT

We walk around so afraid that if the world saw the real us, we wouldn't be impressive enough. Who are we trying to impress anyway? Well, in my line of work, the reality is that I do try to impress people, with what's possible for each of them and how I can help. And at first I was taught that it required me to put out a version of me that was a lot more perfect than the real thing. When I started my business, I listened to the advice of many who had gone before me who err on the side of less reality is more. Make sure everything always looks great to the outside world, they counseled. Don't show the struggle or the failures or the doubts. People won't join you in business if your life doesn't look so much better than theirs. And never leave the house without looking fabulous and dressing to impress.

Thankfully I figured out that a public persona of perfection would leave me too exhausted to run the entrepreneurial marathon and raise two kids. It would suck the joy out of this adventure. And it would make me seem unapproachable and unattainable in a business where anyone can do this, regardless of their professional pedigree, how put together each outfit is, or the size of their ass.

I'll never forget getting stopped in the locker room after a spinning class at the gym one day during my second year in business. There's no doubt I looked pretty bad that day. "Don't you have that skincare business that's helping you and your friends build these big empires?" said a woman I had seen around town but didn't know. Her voice was undeniably tinged with sarcasm. "You're so brave. If beauty were my business, I couldn't go out like that."

Yes, she said that. Out loud.

Ah, at yet another crossroads. I chose real. Really real. "Oh, I am one tired mama," I told her. "One of my kids was up all night, my mom's not well, and I've got PMS from hell. But I'm so proud of myself for getting here today to do something for me—I'm proud of all of us," I said as I gestured to the others in the locker room. And then I added, "Can you imagine how shitty I'd look today if my skincare wasn't so amazing?"

The woman must not have had a good response because she stammered something unintelligible and made a beeline for the showers. However, the woman sitting on the bench next to us had something to say. "I sure love how you handled that," she said. "I had one of those days last week, so I feel you. You have a skincare business? I'd love to hear about it."

She ended up joining my team, because she loved the idea that she could be a hot, busy mess and build something of her own too. I'm not advocating always going out in the world looking like someone who hasn't slept and pulled her wrinkled workout clothes out of the laundry hamper. But on those days you put the "hot" in hot mess, own it. Because on those days, that's the authentic you.

Another good friend and team member, Tracy Willard, started to connect with people on an entirely different level when she stopped shying away from her truth. I like to say that in our business we're paid storytellers, and the better we are at telling our stories—including our backgrounds and why we decided to start our businesses—the more successful we'll be. And I've learned this undeniable truth over the years: the more authentic our stories, the more powerfully we'll connect with others. When Tracy started telling her whole, unfiltered story, that's when she touched people on a deep emotional level and took her business to a new level.

Tracy's husband, Scott, started a new business right at the start of the Great Recession, leaving her family to get by on her low-paying job teaching at the local university. With bills mounting and more month than money, Tracy had to go to the food bank to feed her two girls. They were forced to sell their home in a short sale to avoid foreclosure, and they moved in with her in-laws. It was one fateful day when Tracy was on the floor of her closet crying and praying to God for help—help with her finances; her marriage, which was suffering from the stress; and her feelings of hopelessness. She dried her eyes and went for a walk. She ran into a friend, Nicole, and after a short chitchat, Tracy learned that Nicole (my very first team member) had recently quit her job because of the success of her new business. In what Tracy sees as a sign from God, she kicked off a business that would not only get her family out of dire straits but also transform their entire lives.

But in the first several months of her business, this isn't the story she told people. Instead, she used a sanitized version of needing more income to supplement her teaching salary because "we all know how expensive kids are." While she was growing, I couldn't help but think that her real, unfiltered story would be more powerful, not just for the listener but for herself too. Tracy was understandably hesitant to be that vulnerable and unsure how to navigate her feelings of shame. I encouraged her to muster the same courage it took for her to get up off the closet floor to speak her truth, and we both agree it's been instrumental in her reaching the top levels of our business and one of the most beloved stories.

"Once I was honest and open about my life experience, people were more trusting and open about theirs. There was so much more depth to the conversations I was able to have about what people's lives looked like, what they wanted and needed to change, and whether or not I could help them," Tracy remembers. "My business also became more fun and successful because I was stepping into my truth. Life is better when we share the real—even when it's hard and messy and scary and ugly and beautiful, because that's what everyone's lives are made of."

Even after all my years of trying to lead with authenticity, I'm constantly reminded that I need to stay vigilant and do it more often. There was a week a few months ago where my work had me doing a lot of photos and videos on social media. My hair wasn't "done," I didn't have much more than lip gloss on, and I was either in athleisure wear or a T-shirt and jeans I had grabbed. A week of looking more hot mess-ish wasn't intentional. It was simply my life that week. I was working my ass off in my business, finishing this book proposal, and juggling a million kid demands. Doing anything with my outsides wasn't a Priority, but still getting my messages out there was.

I was shocked by how many people thanked me for looking "so real." Am I the only one who thinks it's crazy that we have to thank one another for actually showing all parts of ourselves, gray roots, unfilled-in brows, and all? In my full life I've worked so hard to get to be all parts of me. I get to be glammed up in Cannes, France, and also work from home, bare-faced with a messy bun and jean cut-offs, taking breaks to pick up dog poop. And I'm so grateful that I figured out it was OK to embrace all parts of me.

If we're just showing each other the highlight reel on and off social media, how will we ever inspire one another? It's so much easier for us to throw up an excuse of "Their life is perfect and mine never will be. That's why they're so successful and I shouldn't even try." It's the biggest, most common cop-out we women use.

We're trying to somehow legitimize, validate, defend, and define our lives and our choices. But what if we stopped looking for the external validation to confirm that how we choose to live is OK, that our imperfections are allowed? And what if we all made a solemn vow to one another and ourselves that we're going to stop showing the highlight reel and instead show all parts of our lives, both online and offline?

HOW TO STAY IN AUTHENTICITY

Here's something so great to remember: we give ourselves clues when we're living inauthentically. The next time you feel out of sync, out of sorts or unhappy, unfulfilled, bored, stressed, uninspired, or stuck, stop and get quiet so you can hear your Heart Voice. It will likely tell you that you're not doing or being what you really want. You're not living your truth.

The more we give ourselves permission to live in authenticity, the more we'll step into our power and purpose and the easier it gets to stay in authenticity, creating a snowball effect that is so large that it becomes habit to make decisions through the lens of "Is this really me? Is this what I want?" Better and easier decisions, more effectiveness. More peace.

Let's face it, it takes a hell of a lot less energy to live your life as you than as someone else. And people can smell bullshit miles away, so why bother? We've already established that our most valuable possession is time, so why waste so much of it not being real?

When I stopped trading in my authenticity for approval, the more I let me be me in all aspects of my life. The more I found my people, the more I found my purpose, the more effective I was in serving others, the more success I experienced. It also made it easier for me to figure out the Priorities and Goals that were important to me and to delete or delegate all the Shoulds.

I have no doubt that without authenticity I couldn't have created a life in which I Have It All. *My* All. And neither can you.

Ten

PRACTICE
FORGIVENESS

*It's one of the greatest gifts you can
give yourself, to forgive.*

—Maya Angelou

There's been so much written about the art of forgiving others and how to release ourselves from the prison of anger, hurt, and resentment. No doubt, practicing forgiveness toward others is essential to free up that energy and emotion for the things that serve us. As the late Carrie Fisher said, "Resentment is like drinking poison and waiting for the other person to die." But I don't want to talk about letting go of grudges we're holding against others.

I want to talk about how we must forgive ourselves.

When I think about how much time I've spent in my life obsessing about and beating myself up for the mistakes I've made, it's just plain sad. So much wasted time, energy, and emotions that have made me doubt myself and question my worthiness. And it's stolen my Focus from what I've declared is really important to me.

Why are we so effing hard on ourselves? Somewhere along the way, we started to believe that we're not supposed to make mistakes or that somehow there are other humans who are anointed at birth with immunity from screwing up, coming up short, or falling flat. But here's the thing: none of us are immune from failure. The point is to use the failures to help propel us forward, and then to learn to practice gratitude for the lessons. I'm not saying it's easy, but with practice we can let go of the grudges we hold against ourselves and grow from what our missteps can teach us.

We're wired to obsess about our screw-ups. Because of what's called the negativity bias, our brains remember negative memories better than positive ones. So the speech you botched, the biz goal you missed, and the argument with your friend where you hit below the belt will have a greater and lasting effect on your psyche than those times—no matter how numerous—when you hit it out of the park.

Research shows that we not only can learn to forgive, but when we do, it can help us improve our mental, emotional, and physical health. The Stanford Forgiveness Project trained 259 adults in forgiveness during a six-week course. Seventy percent of the participants reported a decrease in their hurt feelings, and more than a quarter had fewer physical complaints, like pain, gastrointestinal upset, and dizziness. Another study showed that people who genuinely forgive another for wrongdoing had lower blood pressure and a lower level of the stress hormone cortisol than those who didn't.

So it stands to reason that those of us walking around with feelings of guilt, regret, blame, shame, and even self-hatred for our transgressions and failures have a lot to gain from forgiving ourselves.

Before we can even think about going through the process of forgiving ourselves, we've got to accept that we are not supposed to be perfect. If that's the standard we're holding ourselves up to, we'll never genuinely forgive ourselves for constantly failing to achieve this unattainable goal. I've learned as a wife, parent, daughter, sister, friend, entrepreneur, author, and living, breathing human that we can't learn how to do anything really well without making mistakes. As a recovering perfectionist, I know that if we're shooting for flawless, it will keep us from taking risks or pulling the trigger on projects and make us hold back from putting ourselves out there in a variety of meaningful ways. When I stopped trying to be perfect and instead Focused on trying, doing, exploring, and living, that's when my life got really good. And, as you've already read, it allowed my evolution in authenticity to happen.

Living with a "mistakes happen" mentality is only part of forgiving ourselves. The other essential part, I've learned, is going through a process that allows each misstep to teach us more about who we are. I've learned a lot from my successes, but I've learned a hell of a lot more from my failures. And if you allowed yourself, you can too.

As soon after a stumble as possible, I go through a process that's worked like a charm for me for several years now.

REVIEW. REVISE. RELEASE.

Review requires us to think about what happened and why. This is hard because it forces us to relive what happened and risk feeling the guilt, regret, pain, and/or shame again. But it's the only way for us to get to the good stuff about the times we flop—what we can learn from them. The why part is especially important because it gives us the clues we need to avoid repeating the behavior.

Revise prompts us to problem solve about how we can avoid repeating the same behavior.

Release commands us to let it go—that it happened and all the icky emotions around it. If you do the first two steps, this one is actually possible because you've faced the pain head-on and found the lessons to be learned.

Here's an example of how it works.

When I've yelled at our kids, I've used this process to stop beating myself up that I'm a horrible mom. In reviewing my actions, I figured out that I was bringing the stress of my day into my interactions with them, and that was causing me to lose my shit over the things they did or didn't do. I knew I needed to revise how I was transitioning into my time with them, which is why I started spending five quiet minutes breathing. When I inhaled calm and peace and exhaled whatever I found stressful, I could be the fresher, calmer mom they deserve and respond more appropriately when they do things that frustrate the hell out of me.

Consistently going through this process has shown me patterns. So many of my fails happen if I'm overtired, which keeps me from being as effective or rational or measured as I'd like to be. This makes for yet another compelling argument for me to keep my habit of getting enough sleep. When I say things I shouldn't, I've found it's almost always because I'm hurt and forgetting Ruiz's Second Agreement: "Don't Take Anything Personally." And when I make a bad decision, it's almost invariably because I haven't listened to my Heart Voice, which amplifies my need to have daily doses of quiet. (Hopefully you're seeing that all the stuff I've been talking about is really coming in handy.)

An important part of releasing what we're beating ourselves up for is apologizing to the people we've wronged. When I've yelled at the kids, as soon as I'm able to, I tell them I'm sorry for yelling, that it wasn't OK, and why I think it happened. "No, you shouldn't have left your backpacks, shoes, water bottles, and socks in the middle of the floor, but I shouldn't have yelled. I've had a frustrating day, and I took it out on you. Please forgive me." Whether or not they forgive me—thankfully, they always say they do—I can forgive myself and let it go.

Bebe is starting to be open to this process, and Nate—who's often hard on himself (apple and tree)—uses it often. I delight in the fact that he's going to avoid wasting so much of his precious life beating himself up.

Over the years, among the many, many things I've forgiven myself for:

My many eff-ups in relationships.

That I was a crappy employee because I didn't love my profession and not being my own boss.

Snapping at my husband when he didn't deserve it.

The ten pounds I've gained and lost and regained, again and again.

The chances I didn't take because I was scared.

The things I said in the moment out of anger or because I was hurt.

The things I didn't say to stand up for myself.

There's no time like the present to start using a tool. Write down all the things you're holding as grudges against yourself. Be brave enough to make yourself feel the feelings, and then go through the three R's process. Finally, write down the person or people you need to apologize to in order to forgive yourself.

I need to forgive myself for

....

....

Review: What happened and why?

....

....

Revise: How can I prevent this from happening in the future?

....

....

Release: Who deserves an apology, and when and how will I do it?

....

....

If you have more to forgive, keep writing in your journal or on a separate sheet of paper.

Moving forward, I encourage you to take yourself through this process as soon after one of your inevitable eff-ups as possible, to lessen the emotional and physical toil on you and get to the golden nuggets of learning as quickly as possible. I often find I'm the most open to the three R's after a workout or my quiet time, because my head tends to be the clearest and calmest.

LETTING GO OF WHAT WE'RE NOT

The other part of forgiveness that's essential is forgiving ourselves for all the things we're not. In coaching thousands of women, I've been amazed by how many of us have a really hard time coming up with a long list, or any list at all, when asked what we do well. Yet we could write a treatise on what we should be doing better.

If we Focus on everything we're not, how can we evolve and grow into all we're designed to be? We can't expect to have the time and energy and brain space for the really important stuff if we're comparing ourselves to our own ridiculous expectations of what we should be and do in every aspect of our lives—mom, wife, professional, cook, fitness devotee, fashionista, scintillating conversationalist, and I could go on and on.

Something magical started to happen in my forties. If you're there, I hope you've experienced it too. If you're younger, perhaps you can be ahead of your years in adopting this mindset. Forty started to unlock an acceptance of everything I'm not and a celebration of everything I am. It was freeing, euphoric even. Now, I'm not saying we should abandon our efforts to work toward being kinder, more productive, healthier, more effective, more attractive (if that's important to you) humans. I'm talking about letting go of the stuff about ourselves that we can't change.

I'm a short, sturdy, and curvy woman who is so over beating myself up for not being a size 2 with long and lithe limbs. I'm not crafty. Or good at spatial relations. Or capable of eating just one French fry. This is just a partial list of many things I'm not. And I'm OK with it all—finally—because I choose to Focus on and celebrate all the things I am. Like insanely hardworking, fiercely loyal, able to make people laugh, capable of unconditional love, and I could go on and on.

I want you to go on and on about all the things that you love about you, that you're good at, that you offer your family, coworkers, and community.

I love that I am

....

....

....

....

....

Hopefully your list shows you that your lack of thigh gap or culinary skills aren't quite as important as you thought. I encourage you to revisit this love list of yours whenever you need a shot of confidence or a reminder of all you are. I hope that as you continue to take risks and grow that the list of things you love about yourself grows too.

If we refuse to forgive ourselves for our screw-ups, over time we'll stop taking the risks required to be more, do more, and serve more. If we're Focusing our energy on past events we can't control, it's a waste of our precious energy. It's not moving us closer to our goals but rather keeping us mired in our past. And who the hell has time for that? Plus, the relationship we have with ourselves mirrors the one we have with others. If we can't have grace with ourselves, we can't possibly expect to have it with anyone else.

All of us do our very best with the feelings and knowledge and limited experience we have at any given time. If we want to truly Have It All, we must see our mistakes as opportunities that have been given to us to help us grow. Once we know better, we do better. Now go forth and fuck up with gusto, knowing there's so much to be learned!

#FFEAR

*It's not our job to argue with fear or fix it or
escape it. It's our job to act in spite of it.*

—Romi Neustadt

You can read or listen to hundreds of phenomenal books about how to live a more intentional and fulfilling life, and I hope by now you think this is one of them. But all the strategies, tools, and tips I've given you to this point aren't going to help if you allow your Focus to be distracted, deflated, or derailed by a four-letter word.

FEAR.

We humans all have fears, and there's no way to escape it. I'll never forget when John and I watched our then five-year-old daughter, Bebe, in her first dance recital. Her little confident self, along with her fellow dancers, pranced and strutted all over that stage. They didn't remember all the steps. They certainly didn't carry out flawless performances. But they danced their little hearts out, with unbridled enthusiasm. With pure joy. Without fear. Yes, they were very proud of the costumes they were wearing, but what really struck me is that they were naked little souls. They were how God and the Universe intended them to be.

See, at their age, no one has told them yet that they're not naturally talented, or that they shouldn't try to dance because they'll never be one of the few to make it on Broadway. No one's told them they're not pretty enough. Or tall enough. Or thin enough. Or that dancing isn't a respectable endeavor. And they don't have a track record of other disappointments or failures to squash their confidence. They're just dancing to the music simply because one day they decided they wanted to dance.

Fast-forward a couple of years to when Bebe's passion had advanced to the competitive troupe. The reckless abandon had already been tempered by a system that ranks and judges, has winners and losers. Her rehearsals, both in the studio and in her bedroom, had a new observer: Self-Doubt. She was already wondering at seven years old: Am I good enough? Can I do this? What if I fail? What will people think?

This is what happens to all of us. We experience disappointments. And failures. And rankings. And unsupportive relationships. Life happens, and we get cloaked in fear. Over time it can become so thick and heavy that it keeps us from remembering our dreams or daring to dream new ones. We limit our idea of what we're capable of, and we let go of who we're meant to be. It gives birth to voices in our heads that become so loud that we can't hear the real us anymore.

One of the greatest gifts of my life is that I have the privilege of touching hundreds of thousands of women through my business. While it's filled my heart to be a part of each of their unique evolutions, it's also broken it to see how many women settle for mediocre because it's easier than going after what they really want. They choose safe over satisfaction. Caution over living free and fulfilled. The reason? They're scared shitless.

In my first book, *Get Over Your Damn Self*, I talked about how fear keeps many of the entrepreneurs I work with from building the businesses they're capable of, in spite of having all the training and resources they could possibly need. It's because fear has drowned out their reasons why they wanted to build something of their own in the first place, rendered the coaching irrelevant and caused them to doubt what they're capable of creating. To prove this point, I shared all the fears reported by a small accountability group of team members I was mentoring. And what's #funnynotfunny is that this long list bubbled out of just thirty women, with the overwhelming majority reporting at least four. You'll see that these women are afraid of damn near everything. Fear of failure *and* fear of success. Fear of not being good enough or being too good. Fear of fear. While some of them are specific to our business, I have a feeling you'll be able to relate to nearly all of them.

- Fear of not saying the right thing
- Fear of looking or sounding stupid
- Fear I'm exuding too much confidence
- Fear I'm not confident enough
- Fear of not being taken seriously
- Fear of what people think of me
- Fear of what people think of this business

- Fear of annoying all my friends and family
- Fear of pestering people
- Fear of being "that person" that everyone wants to run from
- Fear that I don't have what it takes
- Fear of not having the right network
- Fear of exhausting my network
- Fear of running out of people to talk to
- Fear I won't meet new people
- Fear of not finding the right people
- Fear of investing time in the wrong people
- Fear of rejection
- Fear of getting a "No"
- Fear of a "No" changing our relationship
- Fear of being judged
- Fear of disappointing others
- Fear of disappointing myself
- Fear of letting my kids down
- Fear of letting my husband down
- Fear of letting myself down
- Fear of proving my critics right
- Fear of not proving my critics wrong
- Fear of stressing myself out
- Fear of putting too much pressure on myself

- Fear of not going fast enough
- Fear I've gone too fast and will hit a wall
- Fear of really applying myself and failing
- Fear of hitting a plateau and not moving past it
- Fear of not finding business partners
- Fear of not being able to train new business partners
- Fear of not growing a team
- Fear of not being able to lead a team
- Fear of not doing enough for my team
- Fear of not finding people who see what I see
- Fear of the time I've sacrificed and it not being worth it
- Fear of never being able to balance my business with the rest of my life
- Fear of my business getting too big to balance
- Fear of not making enough money
- Fear of making a lot of money
- Fear of success
- Fear of failure
- Fear of my team failing
- Fear of not sustaining success once I get there
- Fear of being good but not great
- Fear of not being efficient enough to grow big
- Fear of having to choose between my current career and this company

· Fear of going all in and then it gets taken away or collapses

· Fear of not being enough for everyone

· Fear of not being a good leader for my team

· Fear of not being as good at mentoring as my mentor

· Fear of the unknown

· Fear of never, ever being able to retire because I was a chickenshit or too tired or too distracted

· Fear of letting "I can't" win over "I can"

So, can you relate?

I wish I had the magic elixir that could help all of us silence our fears talking to us through the negative voices in our heads. But I can't. For us humans, there's no getting rid of fear.

As Elizabeth Gilbert wrote in her epic book *Big Magic*, fear will always show up when we strive for great things and take risks because "fear *hates* uncertain outcome . . . This is all totally natural and human." Fear will always show up when we're embarking on the unknown to become more of the person we were designed to be and to design the life we really want. The goal is not to live without fear; it's to keep a big pile of courage handy to fight the fear.

Nelson Mandela said in one of my all-time favorite quotes: "I learned that courage was not the absence of fear, but the triumph over it. The brave man [*or woman*] is not he [*or she*] who doesn't feel afraid, but he [*or she*] who conquers that fear."

IT'S OUR JOB TO ACT IN SPITE OF IT

I've learned to lean into the fear instead of trying to ignore or escape it. I've learned to recognize fear as a signal that I'm onto something good and on the right path. Because the stuff that scares me is also what's going to push me out of my comfort zone and require me to grow and stretch and be true to myself.

I've learned to #FFEAR, and it's my job to teach you how to do the same. For some of you, the F stands for Fight Fear. And if that's enough to get you to muster the courage and kick what's scaring you into the corner, more power to you, honey. For me, I need something stronger, something more visceral. And by now you know I don't shy away from a well-placed f-bomb. So my battle cry against fear is Fuck Fear. Choose whichever version feels right for you—just use it! And I hope that by the end of this chapter you'll not only have the tools to #FFear but also a desire to talk about your triumphs with those you love and work with and connect with on social media. Because the more we talk about our fears and every time we don't let them win, the more we'll inspire one another to choose courage. Because that's when the magic happens.

And let's teach our kids to #FFEAR too so that they learn to find their courage earlier. I've loved every time that Nate and Bebe have said #FFEAR before going onstage, before a test, or before getting stitches.

My life is filled with examples of when I let fear win. From the career choices I made because I didn't think I was good enough to go after what I really wanted. To the boundaries I didn't set and the people I allowed to stay in my life longer than they deserved to be because I was afraid to be judged. The self-care I didn't allow myself because I was afraid I wouldn't have the time to get through my to-do list. And all the Shoulds I said yes to because I feared what others would think about me if I said no. Hell, I even chose my phone over real people who were important to me in the real world because I was afraid of what I'd miss if I wasn't constantly plugged in.

But when I mustered the courage to act in spite of my fears, it was because my desire to grow, stretch, dream, and achieve was far greater. The fears didn't disappear. I just learned to say, "Fuck fear, I'm doing this." Was it scary to leave a career that didn't fit me (lawyer) and a city that didn't feel right (Dallas) to go find myself professionally and personally in New York without a job and a place to live? Absolutely. But my desire to take a big bite out of the Big Apple and devour more of my life far outweighed my fear of the unknown.

Was I scared to start a side business in the direct selling channel after more than twelve years of successful, respected, award-winning public relations work? You bet. But my dreams of the life I really wanted were so much bigger than my fears of failing and what others would think.

Was it terrifying for this former control freak to delegate to others? Yes, but it terrified me more to think that I wouldn't have time for all the things that were important to me. Was it scary for this type A people pleaser to start relentlessly redlining my commitments? Yep, but I ultimately decided that I cared a lot more about living my truth and serving my Priorities than pleasing others.

I make my living having conversations—one-on-one and in front of groups. If I had Focused on the chance that what came out of my mouth wouldn't be perfect, I never would've opened it in the first place. And what a shame that would have been, not just for me and my family but for all the people I've been able to touch in some way. If I had Focused on the possibility that my first book wouldn't be any good, I never would have let my fingers type a bestseller that's helped hundreds of thousands and funded kids' literacy projects. And you sure as hell wouldn't be reading this book right now.

Yes, I have a long history of taking a deep breath, trusting my gut, and pushing through my fears to get to the really good stuff. And it's required more than a mere declaration to summon the courage.

HOW TO #FFEAR

Doing the scary stuff never gets easier. I think we just get stronger. But until you build up that strength, it's helpful to have a process that a therapist taught me years ago to call BS on our fears. I've used it countless times on myself, those I coach, our kids, my mom, and my friends. Think about it: all the fears that I've talked about, that my thirty mentees listed and the majority of you grapple with, are emotion talking instead of fact. So, if we can recognize where the emotion is coming from and counter it with fact, it makes it easier to muster courage.

You've already seen that I'm a big fan of habits, and I want you to adopt the habit of leaning into your fears and labeling them, instead of silently sitting with them as they block you from living the life you want. Because once we call them out, we can tell them to shut the eff up and go sit in the corner while we get on with the business of being unapologetically ourselves, slaying our goals and enjoying a continual evolution as a badass in the process.

Here are the steps:

1. Identify the fear.

2. Ask yourself why you're afraid. This is where courage starts to kick in because you've got to be brave enough to get real about the reason(s) behind your fear.

3. Ask yourself what's the worst possible thing that could happen, taking it to the most awful outcome, no matter how farfetched.

4. Declare what you know to be true; in other words, take emotion out of it and Focus on the facts.

5. Ask yourself what's the best possible outcome. This requires you to tell yourself a different story. Instead of Focusing on fear, you Focus on possibilities.

It may seem obvious to go through this exercise with "big things," like starting a business or throwing your hat in the ring for a speaking opportunity. And it works beautifully for those things. But I want to give you examples of how to use this process to #FFEAR and do the very things I've talked about in this book to help you Have It All.

Here's an example:

I'm afraid to say no to cochairing the school fundraiser.

What are you afraid of?

I'm afraid of what people will think.

What's the worst thing that could happen?

The other cochair and the women at school might think I'm a total bitch and stop talking to me and stop their kids from playing with my kid.

What do you know to be true?

They'll get someone else to do it.

What's the best thing that could happen?

I can use the time I would've spent on the fundraiser to achieve my Goal of [growing my business by 15 percent or running the half-marathon or spending more time playing with my kids].

When you Focus on the factual outcome of your action—and not the catastrophic BS story you make up in your head—it becomes much easier to #FFEAR and muster the courage to do what's best for you, which might be using the time to achieve a Goal that serves one of your Priorities.

Here's another one:

I'm afraid to have an earlier bedtime to get more sleep.

What are you afraid of?

I'm afraid I won't get everything done that I need to.

What's the worst thing that could happen?

I'll get fired and my kids won't have anything to wear or eat.

What do you know to be true?

My body needs more sleep.

What's the best thing that could happen?

I'll be more productive if I get more rest. If I delete or delegate some things off my to-do list that aren't serving my Priorities, I'll have the time to get my work done earlier, get done everything I need to Focus on, and get the rest my body needs.

And another:

I'm afraid to pay someone to drive my kids around to afterschool activities.

Why are you afraid?

I'm afraid of how it looks to the other moms if I'm not the one driving, that they'll think I'm a bad mom.

What's the worst thing that could happen?

The moms will talk about me behind my back and post on social media about what a horrible mom I am and make snide comments to my kids that I'm a bad mom and my kids will believe them.

What do you know to be true?

This is the only time I can find to work out.

What's the best thing that could happen?

Because I've taken the time for me and my health, when I'm with my kids for dinner and homework and before bed, I will be more present, calmer, and happier. I'll be able to better connect with them and better cope with the chaos that ensues around bedtime.

Now it's your turn. Get real about three of the fears you're currently facing, identify the emotions, and then Focus on the facts.

Fear

....

....

Why are you afraid?

....

....

What's the worst thing that could happen?

....

....

What do you know to be true?

....

....

What's the best thing that could happen?

....

....

Fear

....

....

Why are you afraid?

....

....

What's the worst thing that could happen?

....

....

What do you know to be true?

....

....

What's the best thing that could happen?

....

....

Fear

....

....

Why are you afraid?

....

....

What's the worst thing that could happen?

....

....

What do you know to be true?

....

....

What's the best thing that could happen?

....

....

See, when we review the facts, it's never as bad and scary as the BS story we're making up in our heads. It's also easier to Focus on what's best for us, what we really want.

BELIEVE IN ENOUGH

If you're going to #FFEAR from here on out, I've got to call out
the scarcity mindset most of us carry around that's fueling our
fears. We're profoundly afraid that we're not enough to do the
things we want to do and be who we were meant to be. We
question whether we're capable and worthy of building a life in
which we get to Have It All. And if all that isn't debilitating
enough, we also question whether we have enough time and energy
and whether there's enough success to go around. Like most fears,
these are fueled by the BS stories we make up in our heads.

When I was breaking out on my own in the world, I chose to
tell myself I wasn't enough to pursue my dreams, so I went to law
school, and that could have become my permanent narrative. Instead, I chose to tell myself the story of what's the best thing that
could happen. That I could leave law and the life I knew to find a
new adventure that fit me better and a profession that would use
my talents and personality. That I could years later start an entrepreneurial journey and would be able to learn all the things I
didn't know and create something of my own on my terms that
would change my life. That I could grab the opportunities that
excited and scared the crap out of me and go all in, doubts be
damned. That I was enough.

I also chose to believe I had enough time. I said yes to adding
a business to my already full plate, to writing two books, and to
all the things that make me feel like a whole and sane and healthy
person. I chose to believe that someone like me could enjoy all
the success I was willing to work for. Because the best thing
that could happen is that the only limits on my dreams would

be the ones I put on them. And I was never going to limit them again.

I've come to learn that each of us has everything we need to become the people we want to be and to live the lives we desire—if and only if we're willing to do the learning and growing and heavy lifting required to get there. I also know that each of us has enough time, if we spend it on the things that we've declared are important to us. We have more than enough energy, if we protect ourselves from everything and everyone who drains us.

DARING TO HAVE IT ALL IS SCARY

You've been procrastinating the decisions you need to make and the actions you need to take. But it's not because you're lazy. It's because you're afraid. Sarah, Emily, Bridget, and Tracy were too. Sarah was afraid of letting people down, Emily afraid of giving in to chaos and losing control, Bridget of being judged for who she is, and Tracy of being judged for being in such a dire predicament.

But ultimately, these inspiring women had an even bigger fear, one that drives me every day. What scares me *most* is not living the life I was meant to live. Not touching the lives I was meant to touch. Not teaching our kids to go after their dreams and live their truth. Maya Angelou wrote, "There is no greater agony than bearing an untold story inside of you." What scares me shitless is getting to the end of my days and not having written *my* story. Not having lived a life with *my All*.

It takes a whole lot of brave to declare what's important to you and to go after it every damn day. It's easier and safer to settle for a lot less than your All. But I've learned that the magic happens when regular people like us choose courage over fear, put one foot in front of the other, and do what our Heart Voices command us to do.

Let's right here, right now make a pact that we're going to make our biggest, loudest fears revolve around this: fear of what we'll miss out on if we don't make different choices, find our voice, be ourselves, and go after our dreams.

I still have fears every single day about my business, my parenting skills, my relationships, my choices. Every time my husband sends an email to one of the kids' teachers, I'm thrilled that I have such an active parenting partner. Yet I still fear the recipient is judging me for not adequately fulfilling stereotypical gender roles. Every day that I sat down to write this book, my anxiety rose as I questioned whether I'm providing you with anything of value. When I stop what I'm doing to grab some quiet time, I still get nervous that a few minutes of self-care may keep me from getting everything done.

Yet I do it all anyway. Because I'll be damned if I'm going to let fear win.

Here's the ultimate question that only you can answer. And the answer will dictate whether you will Have It All. Will you give fear the power over you? Or will you command it to get the hell out of your way so you can once and for all get to the business of becoming all you were meant to be and live the life you want? Not anyone else's, but yours.

Do you have the courage inside you to Have It All? I most certainly know that you do.

Twelve

LOVE YOURSELF

Do you want to meet the love of your life?
Look in the mirror.

—Byron Katie

W̲e women are so good at pouring into everyone and everything else and showering others with love. But in order to Have It All, we have to love ourselves most. Well, that feels weird, doesn't it? Self-indulgent. Wrong.

But it's not. It's what this whole book has been about. I've been teaching you how to love yourself the most. Because declaring our true desires and then doing whatever it takes to make them happen isn't greedy or narcissistic. It's the ultimate expression of love.

If you really want to Have It All, you have to love yourself so much that you're willing to let go of what anyone else thinks, to say no to everyone and everything that's not right for you. To make time for you.

And this love must be unconditional. It can't matter that you're imperfect and walk around with doubts and fears and flaws. It can't depend on what the scale says or the size of your bank account. It can't require a large personal cheering section, because it's not someone else's job to love you or approve of your choices. It's yours.

Imagine if we all truly loved ourselves and made life choices based on our true desires. We'd each feel content, fulfilled, and excited about our own lives, which means we'd be a hell of a lot less concerned with what other women are doing. We'd stop comparing and defending, and we'd stop judging. Imagine all the cheering for one another we'd do as we moved along, feeling secure on our unique journeys. That's a world I want to live in, the world I want for my children. So let's promise one another that we'll keep doing the work to get there.

I want to leave you with some words I wrote for our son last year. Our family traveled to Israel for Nate's dream bar mitzvah. It's customary at a bar or bat mitzvah for the parents to tell their son or daughter some monumental words of wisdom. I now know from experience that this is a lot of pressure, made even greater because I knew that whatever I said wouldn't be just for him but also for his intently listening sister.

After all these months of writing my monumental words of wisdom for you, I guess I'm not surprised that what I told my kids I wish for them are the same things I wish for you. Because whether we're thirteen or thirty-three or sixty-three, where we Focus our time, energy, thoughts, and actions defines our life and who we are.

I hope you Focus less on being perfect and more on taking risks and giving yourself the freedom to fail, because it's in our mistakes, missteps, and full-out failures that we learn the most about life and about ourselves.

I hope you Focus less on doing things to elicit praise and more on doing what will serve your passions.

Focus less on feeding an image of what you think others expect of you and more on feeding your imagination of what you are here to do and what your life can look like.

Focus less on checking the boxes and achieving status and more on the satisfaction that comes from living your truth in all parts of your life.

And may you always remember that the one thing that you have that nobody else has is YOU. Your voice. Your mind. Your heart. Your vision. Nobody else gets to write the story of your life but you, and I know it's going to be one hell of a story.

What I was trying to teach Nate and Bebe is to love themselves enough to put their needs and desires and dreams first. Because when we do, we're able to offer so much more in our relationships, our families, our careers, and our communities. And we're able to live with the joy and fulfillment that only comes when we live in our truth.

No matter what your age and what's happened in your past, you have the power to write your story. I've given you permission to declare what's important to you and to say No to the rest. I've given you tools to make changes, tweaks, edits, and deletions and to determine your worth. I've asked you to forgive yourself and show up as your authentic self in all parts of your life. And I've implored you to get quiet so the voice you hear is your Heart Voice. It will always tell you what to do.

Now it's time for you to embrace your wildest dreams of what you really want your life to look like and to discard everything that isn't serving them. It's time to love yourself fully and unconditionally.

You can Have It All. Just not at the same damn time.

You can do anything. But you can't do everything.

Choose wisely, my Sister. Choose YOU.

Acknowledgments

A n essential key to Have It All is surrounding yourself with the right people. My success, happiness, fulfillment, and growth are a reflection of very important people— whether they're in my life for a season or forever.

I'm filled with gratitude and love for my priceless girlfriends who are on their own journeys to Have It All. Amy Hofer, Bridget Cavanaugh, Holly Brewer, Lori Bush, and Marissa McDonough, your endless encouragement kept me going during the long, scary, lonely, doubting times that come with writing a book, and you made celebrating milestones that much sweeter. I love you, your hearts, your brains, and your wicked senses of humor.

To Amy Bryd, Betzy Lynch, Cathy Fluegel, Christy Nutter, Emily Piniatoglou, Erica MacKinnon, Hannah Fisher, Jamie Petersen, Jen Griswold, Jenn Soine, Kate Hester, Kimmy Brooke, Lauren Myers, Linda Ray, Lisa Ross, Meredith Tieszen, Michelle Kelly, Myisha Procter, Natalie Cruz, Nicole Cormany, Rachael Braunshweiger, Stephanie Sarazin, and Tracy Willard, your cheers and reminders that what I have to say can help others is priceless, as are your friendships. I hope you feel the same support from me that I cherish from you.

To all the women of my Powered by You Team, thank you for letting me into your businesses and your lives, for teaching me so much about the complex struggle to Have It All, and for teaching me so much about myself. A big reason why I continue working to become a better version of me is so I can serve you better.

To Bridget, Daniela, Emily, Holly, Marissa, Sarah, and Tracy, thank you for letting me tell your beautiful stories. You and your authenticity made this book so much better. I'm forever grateful.

I've learned to delegate and have assembled a squad that makes it possible for me to Have It All. I'm not talking about a glam squad (although one of those would be pretty fabulous). I'm talking about a team of people who make my very full life of work, parenting, pets, play, and preserving my marriage possible. They have my deepest gratitude and mad respect:

Ianthe Andress, you kept the wheels on my business bus while I had to Focus more time on this labor of love, and I'm so grateful for your work ethic, attention to detail, ability to juggle, endless cheerfulness, and wicked sense of humor.

Laura, you come into the aftermath of our personal tornado created by two entrepreneurs, two kids, and two dogs, and make it all right again. You clean our toilets and do our laundry, you patiently turn off the vacuum every time I need to film something, and you never openly judge the disaster my office is during big projects like this one. Did I mention you clean our toilets? Thank you.

To Linda Branson, our wife, the COO of our household, and my dear friend. While I typed away, you brought me coffee and sweet peas and watermelon and got our kitchen ready for a remodel. You fill in the many spaces I continue to leave for you to fill, and you love and take care of our kids like your own. You take care of me like your own. I don't know what our family would do without you. I don't know what I'd do without you.

Writing a book is a lonely endeavor, but this time around I didn't have to do it alone. After my first book became a bestseller and it was time for me to find a literary agent, I was told Jim Levine is the absolute best person a nonfiction author can have in her corner. I pinch myself all the time that you loved *Get Over Your Damn Self* and the other things that I have to say so much that you took me on. Thank you for believing in me and for always being as steady, calm, and patient as I am passionate, impatient, and mercurial.

I had no idea what to expect from a publisher, but I hit the jackpot with Portfolio. Thank you for your enthusiasm for this book and your belief in me. To my editor, Niki Papadopoulos, you've made me a better writer, and I love collaborating with you. Thank you for pushing me, playing therapist when it was necessary, and wanting me to be unabashedly me. I'm cheering you on as you figure out how to Have It All.

To Sadie Neustadt, our beloved labradoodle, thank you for once again sprawling yourself around my office floor as I wrote and rewrote away. I'm grateful you kept me company and provided the coziest of footrests.

Mom, this book is about choices that you never had the opportunity to make. Your family was your everything, and I know there was so much more you might have wanted to do, to become. Even though you can't relate to my All, you show so much delight for the life I've built and cheer me on enough for Dad too. I feel appreciated and respected and loved, and I hope I do the same for my kids when they're adults.

To my sister Connie, who helped me in so many ways along my quest to Have It All. Because you're sixteen years older you were not only my big sister; you often assumed the role of another parent. I don't for a minute forget all the things you've done for me and my family. What I treasure most are the beautiful memories of us being sisters, laughing until we couldn't breathe over waxing and pies and Dustin Hoffman. What I wish for you—what I've always wished for you (even back when I snuck my silver dollar collection into your luggage)—is that you have all you want, that you're fulfilled and happy and surrounded by love.

Of course I have to thank Oprah for being, well, *Oprah*. What she said all those years ago got me all fired up and wanting to prove her wrong. And everything else I've ever heard her say has led me to countless Aha Moments on my journey to become the person I was designed to be and live the life I want to live. I hope to sit with you one day and talk about life, how to Have It All, and what we both know for sure.

And no matter what else in life I achieve and acquire, the most important parts of my All are the three people who hold my heart.

Nate and Bebe, thank you for understanding that my Goal of writing this book meant that sometimes I had to let go of my Goal of spending quality time with you every day. Thank you for remembering to ask me how the writing was coming and for every time you let me know that you believed in me. Out of everything I will ever do during my time on Earth, being your mom is the most important and what I'm most proud of. You teach me more about life every day, and you inspire me to evolve into a better person who's worthy of being your mom. I hope this book will one day serve as a guide for you and remind you of all the things I'm trying to teach you as you grow. And I hope it makes up for all the things I'm doing that will land you in therapy.

John Neustadt, there would be no All without you. Thank you for always supporting me and my growth, for picking me up when I fall down, for believing when I doubt, for being my rock, and for loving all of me, even when I'm PMSing from hell. I love that we remain committed to helping each other have our own All, and I thank you for doing more than your share so I could put this out in the world. The last time I wrote a book it was just you and me, and your edits took it from good to great. This time, even with a big-time publishing house, I still needed your edits to make it better. Just like you make my entire life better. Thank God I found you, Love of My Life.

And I must give props to myself, for not being full of shit and actually doing all the things I write about in this book while writing it. I had to say No to a whole lot to get this baby done on time. Here's a partial list of the things I didn't Focus on:

Cooking dinner. Not once.

Making it to every one of our kids' events. Not even close.

Daily showers. Special props go out to Mum deodorant and dry shampoo.

Attending that mindful parenting series that I really could use but know will be offered again. Because parents everywhere are trying to find the minds they have lost.

The best part is, I'm not beating myself up for any of it. Not even for the fact that my ass has spread and dropped. Because for the last four months, a high, firm ass hasn't been one of my Goals. But watch out, Peaches, I'm coming for ya.

Notes

11 **as few as 8 percent:** "New Years Resolutions Statistics," Statistic Brain Research Institute, December 7, 2018, https://www.statisticbrain.com/new-years-resolution -statistics.

31 **nearly four in ten:** Amanda Dixon, "The Average Side Hustler Earns over $8K Annu-ally," Bankrate.com, June 25, 2018, https://www.bankrate.com/personal-\finance/smart -money/side-hustles-survey-june-2018.

55 **give our brains a hit of dopamine:** Sören Krach et al., "The Rewarding Nature of So-cial Interactions," *Frontiers in Behavioral Neuroscience* 4, no. 22 (May 28, 2010), https://www.ncbi.nlm.nih.gov/pmc/articles/PMC2889690.

65 **women are twice as likely:** "Depression in Women," Mental Health America, accessed January 23, 2019, http://www.mentalhealthamerica.net/conditions/depression-women.

102 **significantly decrease our brain's ability:** For a wealth of information about how technology is screwing up our sleep, read John Neustadt, ND, "Why You Can't Sleep & What to Do About It," Nutritional Biochemistry, Inc., https://nbihealth.com/why-you -cant-sleep-what-to-do-about-it.

105 **40 percent less productive:** "Multitasking: Switching Costs," American Psycholo-gical Association, March 20, 2006, http://www.apa.org/research/action/multitask.aspx; D. M. Sanbonmatsu et al., "Who Multi-Tasks and Why? Multi-Tasking Ability, Perceived Multi-Tasking Ability, Impulsivity, and Sensation Seeking" *PLoS ONE* 8, no. 1 (2013): e54402.

105 **significantly worse on simple memory tasks:** Melina R. Uncapher and Anthony D. Wagner, "Minds and Brains of Media Multitaskers: Current Findings and Future Direc-tions," *Proceedings of the National Academy of Sciences of the United States* 115, no. 40 (October 2018): 9889–96; DOI:10.1073/pnas.1611612115.

106 **goals at the same time:** Jennifer Aaker, "Rethinking Time: The Power of Multipliers," Stanford VMware Women's Leadership Innovation Lab, accessed February 16, 2019, https://womensleadership.stanford.edu/time.

113 **"When you start a new habit":** James Clear, *Atomic Habits* (New York: Avery, 2018), 162.

115 **66 days**: Phillippa Lally et al., "How Are Habits Formed: Modelling Habit Formation in the Real World," *European Journal of Social Psychology* 40, no. 6 (October 2010): 998–1009, https://doi.org/10.1002/ejsp.674.

115 **"There is nothing magical"**: Clear, *Atomic Habits*, 146–47.

120 **"The thought process"**: Cal Newport, *Digital Minimalism* (New York: Portfolio, 2019), 19.

121 **the more we depend on our smartphones**: Adrian F. Ward et al., "Brain Drain: The Mere Presence of One's Own Smartphone Reduces Available Cognitive Capacity," *Journal of the Association of Consumer Research* 2 no. 2 (April 2017): 140–54, https://doi.org/10.1086/691462.

123 **lacking in relationship skills**: Victoria L. Dunckley, "Gray Matters: Too Much Screen Time Damages the Brain," *Psychology Today*, February 27, 2014, accessed February 18, 2019, https://www.psychologytoday.com/us/blog/mental-wealth/201402/gray-matters-too-much-screen-time-damages-the-brain.

130 **"Is this the best way"**: Newport, *Digital Minimalism*, 32.

134 **our "attention resources" get depleted**: Stephen Kaplan, "The Restorative Benefits of Nature: Toward an Integrative Framework," *Journal of Environmental Psychology* 15, no. 3 (September 1995): 169–82.

134 **our brains can restore**: Ibid.

134 **periods of daily silence**: Imke Kirste et al., "Is Silence Golden? Effects of Auditory Stimuli and Their Absence on Adult Hippocampal Neurogenesis," *Brain Structure & Function* 220, no. 2 (March 2015): 1221–28; DOI: 10.1007/s00429-013-0679-3.

134 **just two minutes without stimuli**: L. Bernardi, C. Porta, and P. Sleight, "Cardiovascular, Cerebrovascular, and Respiratory Changes Induced by Different Types of Music in Musicians and Non-Musicians: The Importance of Silence," *Heart* 92, no. 4 (April 2006): 445–52.

159 **struggles we'd had**: If you want to read the blog about some major #MomTruth, go to https://www.romineustadt.com/post/major-momtruth-coming-to-you.

168 **our brains remember**: Roy F. Baumeister et al., "Bad Is Stronger Than Good," *Review of General Psychology* 5, no. 4 (December 2001): 323–70; DOI: 10.1037/1089-2680.5.4.323.

168 **people who genuinely forgive**: Everett L. Worthington Jr. and Michael Scherer, "Forgiveness Is an Emotion-focused Coping Strategy That Can Reduce Health Risks and Promote Health Resilience: Theory, Review, and Hypotheses," *Psychology & Health* 19, no. 3 (2004): 385–405.

Printed in the United States
by Baker & Taylor Publisher Services